Acting Career Start-up

Acting Career Start-up

Four Key Factors For Success

How To Take Control Of Your Career
And Position Yourself For Success Right
From The Start!

By Anthony Smith:
Entrepreneur, Actor, Motivational Speaker and
Former Fortune 500 Company Senior Manager

iUniverse, Inc.
New York Lincoln Shanghai

Acting Career Start-up
Four Key Factors For Success

iUniverse books may be ordered through booksellers or by contacting:

iUniverse
2021 Pine Lake Road, Suite 100
Lincoln, NE 68512
www.iuniverse.com
1-800-Authors (1-800-288-4677)

The views expressed in this work are solely those of the author and do not necessarily reflect the views of the publisher, and the publisher hereby disclaims any responsibility for them.

The author wishes to thank those who have generously given permission to print excerpts from, and make references to their previously published material:

Awaken The Giant Within: How to take immediate control of your mental, emotional, physical & financial destiny! by Anthony Robbins. Copyright © 1991 by Anthony Robbins. All Rights Reserved. Published by Fireside Publishers, New York, NY.

The Seven Habits Of Highly Effective People: Restoring Character Ethic by Stephen R. Covey. Copyright © 1989 by Stephen R. Covey. All Rights Reserved. Published by Fireside Publishers, New York, NY.

www.nikebiz.com. Copyright © 2007 by Nike Inc. All Rights Reserved

ISBN: 978-0-595-41902-9 (pbk)
ISBN: 978-0-595-86250-4 (ebk)

Printed in the United States of America

THANKS TO:

Jackie and Jerry: for always believing in me. Joshua for being my life source of inspiration and for putting up with his father being on the road. Cristina for her continuous support and understanding. Peter Foggin, my teacher and mentor, for introducing to me the wonderful world of facilitating. Laura Brunelli for stimulating my mind to always see different points of view. Laura Lockwood for her friendship and for inspiring me to write this book. Nike Inc., the company I still love and miss, for providing me with an incredible schooling and way of living. Charlie Denson, a man I respect a great deal for his leadership and for all the things he's taught me about business. Gary DeStefano for teaching me about leadership and a concept I carry with me to this day: 'Big Ideas'. Rosario Fiorello for allowing me to get a closer look at show business. The Princess, my special friend, who came into my life to show me a beam of light and to awaken me. Jarod and Cheryl for allowing me into their home and to live first hand the life of working actors. Wendy Ward, my teacher, who has helped me make strides in my acting craft. Janice Hoffmann, one of my coaches, who always provides great input and stimulates my thinking. Grant Neale, for asking us that great question: "How many different ways are there…?" Dr. Gene Carpenter, for his wisdom and for teaching me, through football, how to win at the game of life. Bernard Hiller, the great motivator. April Webster for her input and feedback with regard to my potential as an Actor. Mark S. Levitt for making me understand the importance of sharing my knowledge in book form. Roberto Re for teaching me about the business of training and about marketing myself in my own business. My class of the summer of 2005 at the Ward Studio in New York: Merel, Teres, Lee, Janet, Marion, Nathalie, Elizabeth, Yelena, Grant, Antonio, Vicki. Robert Presley, a hard-working actor, for his friendship and contributions to this book. Ingrid French Management, a great person with whom it is a pleasure to work, for her professionalism, encouragement and support. Brian O'Neil for sharing his wealth of information and for helping me to plan for my success. Lisa Gold for creating a great resource for actors (The Actors Connection), without which I might not have achieved the results I have thus far. Again to Wendy Ward and Janice Hoffman for their support and written contributions to the book. Karen and Katie for helping me crystallize whom this book can benefit most. And to the many actors I have come in contact with over the last three years, who have made me understand that the information in this book is exactly what we aspiring actors need to have a real chance at being successful in this very competitive industry.

CONTENTS

Key Factor #1:
Clarity of Vision:
Figuring Out What You Really Want

Key Factor #2:
Creating The Necessary Motivation:
Making Things Happen!

Key Factor #4
Basic Business Skills:
You The Actor. You The Company. You The Business.

Putting It Into Practice:
A First Hand Account

Before we get into the meat of the book, I want to hand you over to someone who has a lot more experience as an actor than I do. She is a joy to watch on stage and in front of the camera, in a commercial, in a play, or on a daytime soap. She can interpret a range of different roles that most of us can only dream about. We became friends a few years ago when we were chosen to do a scene together in a scene study class. At the time, I was about as green as one can be, because I was just beginning my journey on the path to becoming an actor. I learned so much from her in those six weeks as we rehearsed, and we developed a special friendship that has endured over the past few years, in spite of the distance between Bologna, Italy, and New York City.

Many books have a preface or a foreword, oftentimes written by some well-known person. Most often, though, it is written by someone who is special and who knows the book's author very well, as in this case. I asked Laura to write the preface because she is my muse, my inspiration. Without her input, I'm not sure I would have written the book, at least not right now. I talked with her about many of the things that you will read in this book. And since I wrote it for actors and artists in general, I thought it would be very fitting to have "one of us" introduce the book to you. And so here she is, Laura Lockwood.

PREFACE

Your body is your temple, right? As artists, we know we are supposed to nurture ourselves physically and spiritually so we can be the best we can be. But when it comes to nurturing our careers, many artists find that foggier terrain to tread. What if we knew how to treat our careers with the same sacred care we give our craft? Imagine what we could do!

A while back, Anthony Smith and I sat in Starbuck's sipping hot java and tea while exchanging (sharing, hashing out) ideas about what actors can do to advance their careers. Anthony had a plethora of ideas. He talked about the importance of establishing clear goals and having a means of determining your destination, while charting a clear road map for getting there. He also talked about using effective and simple techniques for problem solving and "thinking outside the box," while never accepting "I don't know" as an answer when pursuing solutions to a career quandary—or a personal one, for that matter! He said something else to me that made a lot of sense. He said with the competition being as great as it is, that if all of us do the same things to get noticed and to get work, then it will be very difficult to stand out. His idea was that, to increase our chances we need to be innovative in our approach, something that once again he learned as part of his successful business background.

I would deem that Starbuck's powwow with Anthony a real coaching session. He enabled me to see that I had a renewed ability to shake things up and claim a different, clearer set of priorities and goals when approaching my own acting career. This, of course, was just the tip of the iceberg. If Anthony could show me how to better empower myself over green tea, what could he do for other actors and artists in general?

I told Anthony that, with his wisdom and ability, he should think about translating his life and business experience into the strengthening of an actor's career; he should do seminars, write a book, be a career coach—he really had a gift.

Several years ago, upon the referral of a trusted fellow actor, I paid an acting career coach a healthy amount of money for a thirty-minute session. What this coach told me was to buy various trade publications, such as *Backstage*, the *Ross Reports*, *Variety*, and so on. When I told him that I was already doing this, he told me I'd have to come to the next session (translation: pay for another round) and get the next bit of valuable info. I felt cheated, and, well, needless to say, I didn't go back.

Being an actor can be full of excitement, change, rebirth, ups and downs, ins and outs, and of course big and little successes. However, when in a stage of transition or in between jobs, actors can feel a bit directionless and out of control of their destiny. In such a fast-paced world, with the need to focus so much on oneself in order to accomplish the goals an artist has before them, it can be hard to find a willing mentor or someone who can dedicate the time to offer counsel or even give a rip, so to speak! (Not to discredit my supportive acting coaches, many supportive friends, and my family, of course, who have fueled me and refueled me so generously.) So what if we don't have an Anthony to have tea with every time we need a healthy dose of career fuel injection? What's one to do?

I believe this book offers this type of assistance. After reading Anthony's book, I was struck by his sincere interest in helping artists achieve their goals and by his ability to clearly, and positively, express his ideas while providing tools that can help artists create new possibilities right now in their careers— and in their lives. He has walked the talk and lived his life according to the philosophies he shares in his book. This book is part of Anthony's fiber, his ideology, and his genuine desire to help artists achieve and thrive.

As an actress who has lived in New York for a number of years, I have, at times, envisioned speaking to high school students who are interested in pursuing a career in the arts. What could I tell them that would help them on their journey? I know many gifted, talented artists whose work should be seen, and yet they have not reached the point in their careers where they can make a living at it. Aside from the lucky breaks that do occur in this industry, for those just beginning their journey as an actor, or for those who are well into it, there can be a missing element common in so many beautiful, talented people—*business savvy*, or the entrepreneurial streak and mental framework of a businessperson; thus, they leave their beautiful gifts perhaps more unnoticed than if they had a business background to complement their acting training. Therefore, I would suggest that young aspiring artists find a way to educate themselves in this area.

You know what they say, "When the student is ready, the teacher appears." I am excited to say that since reading Anthony's book, I started implementing his methods to get ahead and am already seeing results. And not only in my acting career. I've also applied this information to improve the bigger picture, and I must say, it feels so good to be taking more charge of my destiny. I think it is important to understand that we are "artistic entrepreneurs" and that we need to determine and redetermine where we're going with this venture. As all good business owners do, we must constantly evaluate our progress and establish new goals. Having effective tools makes this process more like second nature and saves a lot of time and energy and, yes, money. This is what Anthony's book does for you.

I really wish I had had access years ago to the information contained in this book. I certainly would be further along now, and I wouldn't have made some of the mistakes that I have made. The good thing is that it's never too late, and now I do have access to this information and I'm using it.

So, never fear if you don't have a business background. This book offers invaluable insight based on Anthony's many successful years as a businessman in two fortune 500 companies and now as a creative entrepreneur, actor, and public speaker. His many useful tools for goal setting, career planning, and problem solving (after all, there really are no "problems," only solutions, right?) all come in the form of having a coach that sincerely cares. Anthony's encouragement and insight serve not only as a means to educate yourself and learn some business savvy, but also as an inspiration to "be the person you want to become." Or, perhaps more aptly, this book assists in enabling you to be more of the successful artist you want to become.

I wish you the very best on your journey, from my heart to yours, from one comrade to the other. May success and fulfillment be yours!

Laura Lockwood

INTRODUCTION

Three years ago I made a bold move and left a corporate career after nearly fifteen years to pursue a lifelong dream of becoming an actor, author, speaker, and television host. My situation is a bit complicated in that I'm divorced and have a son I love dearly but who lives with his mother in Italy. At the moment I'm balancing my life between Bologna and New York. I founded a small consulting company in Italy that allows me the flexibility to take off and come to the States for several months out of the year to take acting classes, work the industry, improve my acting and hosting skills, and work. Each time I come back to the States, I put another brick in the foundation of the life that I am building here. I'll be ready to move back soon. After this next trip to New York to finish the next step of my training, my plan is to journey to Los Angeles, where the majority of TV hosting and prime time television work is.

I've learned a lot in these last couple of years, having taken numerous classes, seminars, workshops, and forums with casting directors and agents, and getting feedback and confirmation of my potential and of the fact that I made the right move to pursue what I really love: acting, speaking, television hosting, and writing.

I've come to realize that while television and film acting can be lucrative if one can work continuously, many, many actors and artists are struggling to realize their dreams of "making it" and being able to make a living doing what they love: acting.

In these last three years I've talked with many of my fellow aspiring actors and hosts and find that the people who make up this group of ours have a lot in common.

Why I Wrote This Book

A long time ago I discovered a love for teaching and public speaking. I've worked as a teacher and was also responsible for training and development in a large company. In the military I was responsible for training our squadron's new recruits, and even as a manager, I always strove to develop the people working in my division.

Helping people to improve their quality of life gives me satisfaction. Today, in addition to pursuing acting and hosting, I have my own small company, which trains company managers and employees to improve their performance.

In addition, I also train groups of people from all walks of life who usually want to change some aspect of their lives but don't know how. There are few things that bring greater satisfaction than seeing someone go after their dreams, to do something they never thought they could do, or just begin to be happy for the first time in a long time by doing what they're doing.

I love the craft of acting. I think it is the greatest profession in the world. I love artists and what they stand for. I love the contribution they make to society, how they enrich our lives, tell us stories, teach us, nurture our souls and desires, and help us grow. I have become very attached to this group of human beings, and I want to help make sure that we can all flourish and make our contribution to the human race even greater, more profound, and more meaningful than it already is.

Who Can Benefit Most from Reading This Book?

This book is for Karen and all the young aspiring actors like her. During a recent three-month stay in New York, I met Karen in Brooklyn on the set of the film *Life Support* (starring Queen Latifa) for which we were both cast as extras. While I don't consider myself to be an expert on the business of acting by any stretch of the imagination, I have a great deal more information about this business than Karen, just as there are many actors out there who have a great deal more information than me. Karen is a beautiful young woman, who had driven through the night just to be on the set of this movie. She was so excited, and she talked about wanting to move to New York to seriously pursue modeling and acting. In the same breath, she confided to me, "I'm ashamed to admit it, but if I were to move here, I have absolutely no clue where to start and what to do about anything, getting an agent, working, networking, nothing!" We proceeded to talk at length, and she asked me a multitude of questions and took a lot of notes. I answered them based on my experience and what I had learned and put into practice.

I began to realize in the three months that I was in New York "working the beat" that there are many Karen's out there who have a lot of questions; there are a lot of brand-new actors, hungry for information, hungry for someone to explain to them what their possibilities are and to give them ideas as to what they can do to successfully promote themselves as young artists and, ultimately, to get work.

In my continuous quest for information, I've had many a conversation with working actors. I love to learn, so I pick their brains, ask a lot of questions. The problem is that rarely do those actors have the time to share with me all the details that I would like to know. There are the usual conversations in which all the typical questions are asked and answered: "What do you do? How long have you been acting? What have you booked recently? What agent are you with? Do they send you out a lot? Do you have your SAG/AFTRA cards?" But these are all very superficial questions. You rarely hear about all the *other* things a person does to promote themselves or what they did to land a part, the things that got them to that point, the things that help to make them successful. My background has also trained me to look for the things they do as a person to help them get the results they are getting—their beliefs, their work ethic, their methods, and in general just how they do what they do.

After such a brief conversation, this usually very busy person has to run off before giving you the information that perhaps could have been of most value to you—how they market themselves, how they obtained that agent representation, and what their daily activities are that help them get frequent auditions and consequently book work.

A Little Research

Last year I took a career-mentoring class with a coach named Janice Hoffmann at the Ward Studio in New York that really opened my eyes. Among other things, we talked a lot about the importance of knowing the industry in which we work. This reminded me of my days as a senior manager in Nike, when we talked about that all the time. If you're going to run a successful business, which is precisely what an actor has to do as a freelance professional, you must know the market and you must know the business.

So in this new world of mine—the world of acting and hosting—I was immediately drawn to statistics about the industry that could help me understand more about it. I wanted to find out who exactly I am up against, who my competition is, especially when many people have tried to talk me out of becoming an actor. They said the competition was stiff. I knew that was true. They also said I was up against all the other actors trying to make it. I knew that was not true: I'm in my forties and am a light-skinned African American, often referred to in the industry as ethnically ambiguous. I'm physically fit with a businessman presence, and I'm 6'1" and 180 pounds. Therefore, I know that my competition is not "all the other actors," because we are not all the same type, and we are not all cast for the same roles. Anyway, I went looking for some stats to further my studies of the market.

Among the places I went to for information was the Actors Equity Web site, where I looked at their annual report. This is a great site to find information—to see who is working in theater and what kinds of roles are most sought after, and to see ethnic breakdowns, wages for different types of roles, average earnings, and so on.

The numbers I saw were initially startling, but once I thought about them, they really weren't. For example, I discovered that not long ago, of all the actors registered with the union, the average earnings of Equity members (those who got Equity jobs) were a little more than $6,000 in that year. I realize that many actors, especially those primarily interested in theater, don't earn all their yearly income from acting in Equity-sponsored projects. They need other sources of income, as it is impossible to sustain oneself on $6,000 per year.

I also found an article on the official Web site of the Screen Actors Guild (SAG) about how reality programming has put the squeeze on union roles on episodic television. This led me to believe that the average SAG member probably doesn't make a living from only SAG projects. As a matter of fact, I know many actors who make a living through a mix of Equity, SAG, and AFTRA (Association for Film, Television and Radio Actors).

These excerpts, along with other articles and information I've read, got me thinking more and more about how actors *really* earn a living and just how difficult it can be to pursue this profession! There are many of us who are striving for that coveted role, whether it be in film, in theater, or in prime time or daytime television. So the question for me, and the discussion that emerged between me and my classmates was, "How can we work toward that?"

Doing What It Takes

Coming from thirteen years in the corporate world and three years so far as a corporate consultant, trainer, and motivational speaker, I have been trained to think outside the box. I went to a great school (Nike) where I held positions such as the European sales manager for the military business, the European director of sales training and development, the national sales manager for the Italian subsidiary, and the general manager of the Italian subsidiary of another company. I learned how to be creative and to think about different ways to grow the businesses I was responsible for running. Failure was not accepted. Not trying to come up with a valid approach to achieve company objectives was not accepted. And so I learned that getting good results was the only option available.

To help get great results repeatedly, I learned how fundamentally necessary it is to have a solid method. I learned what this method is, and I use it constantly to achieve results in every area of my life. Many successful people all over the world use this method, and many books have been written about it. This method is proven and works if you follow it. It has the following characteristics.

1. *Clarity of vision.* I've learned that by knowing *exactly* what we want, we are ten times more likely to get it. The more specific we can be in identifying the exact result we are looking to achieve, the more probable it is that we can get it. Do you know exactly what you want and where you want to be in, say, five years?

2. *Creating the necessary motivation* we need to achieve our goals. This can be the trump card. It can make all the difference in the world. Many people think that we either have the drive and motivation to pursue what you want or we don't. I know that is not true. Are you driven, really motivated, unstoppable, determined, tenacious, and on your way to achieving that goal?

3. *Having a solid plan and a method for monitoring that plan* to ensure we stay on track toward achieving our goals dramatically increases our chances of fulfilling our desires. Do you have a solid plan that you have written down and monitor on a daily basis to ensure you stay on track to achieve what you want?

These things are common to anyone who wants to enjoy success in any field. However, with regard to those in a business profession, those who have a product to sell, there are some other very important concepts.

4. These are *the basic principles of success in business.* There are certain principles that, if we know what they are and how best to use them, they can propel us to success in a much shorter time than if we don't know how to use them.

This book addresses these areas in great detail. These things have helped me to be successful throughout my life. They are the things that I have also seen fellow actors and performers successfully apply to their profession. I am sharing them with you. These are also the things that some of the most noted acting industry professionals, casting directors, agents, teachers, authors, and coaches talk about in their work and in their communication to actors. So, that, coupled with my past experience in business, lets me know I'm on the right track.

Which Group Do You Belong To?

In my work as a corporate trainer and consultant, I often talk to groups and senior managers about beliefs and how they influence outcome. That's another reason I wrote this book. I want to share with you some of those fundamentals. I want to impart what I know about modeling successful behavior to get the results you want. This is taken from my own corporate experience and from studying the habits of successful individuals with whom I have worked, about whom I have read, and with whom I have had the privilege of interacting.

There are some additional concepts that are applied in business that I want to share with you. I hope they will inspire you to apply them to managing your own career as an artist. Actors who are successful and who consistently get good results, who are working, those actors who started from scratch were not always just lucky or discovered; rather, they consistently applied these principles, sometimes without even realizing it.

It's true that people who are successful and who get what they want on a regular basis have something in common. It's their attitude, their method, and their process. These methods and way of thinking, which have helped me tremendously throughout my life, can help you, too, if you learn how to access and develop them. They are already inside you, and you need only to pull them out.

There are some people who, no matter what they do, no matter what mission they embark on in life, they are always successful. Do you know anyone like that? You can give them any task and they will make it work. On the other hand, there are some folks who you wouldn't trust to do even the simplest things, because you know their track record isn't very good. They can never seem to get things right. They always need help, have trouble understanding simple instructions, are not very responsible or reliable. Do you know anyone like that?

The people who make up the first group—achievers—have something in common. People who consistently get things done and who achieve great results are clear about what they want; they have a method and an attitude that assists them. They are disciplined and have a strong belief that anything is possible. They are determined and unstoppable. When they don't know how to do something, they find out and they never give up until they get what they want. On the other hand, the people in the other group—the nonachievers—also have things in common that are usually the exact opposite of the characteristics shared by achievers.

I now ask you the first of many questions throughout this book: Which group do you belong to? Are you happy with the results you are currently getting in your career as an actor? Do you believe that it's possible to get better results than you are currently getting? Are you interested in learning a method that, if you apply it, is guaranteed to dramatically increase your chances for success in any field you choose?

Come to the Party

This book is written from a unique point of view, because, while I am already enjoying success as a consultant, seminar leader, motivational speaker, and writer, I, too, am an aspiring actor and TV host, and I, too, have much to learn about this industry.

Sharing this information with other actors, as I do in this book, is like coming to a covered-dish party, where everyone brings a dish they cooked and shares with everyone present. The party I'm talking about here is for actors and artists. I'm bringing the chicken. I love chicken. I'm really good at cooking chicken. I have a lot of experience cooking chicken. I can cook it in different ways: barbecued, grilled, fried, broiled, any way you want. The chicken I'm bringing to this party is *Acting Career Startup: 4 Key Factors For Success.* This is what I know. It's what I have applied and what has gotten me success in my life to date and what has gotten me some success thus far as a performer. It really works when it is applied.

Like I said, I've come to the party with my dish. I'm looking forward to sharing "my chicken" with you and other actors, artists, agents, casting directors, directors, producers, and other industry professionals and tasting the dishes that everyone brings to this party. That way we can all grow. I encourage you to share your information with me and with other actors. In this way, I hope to grow and achieve the success I want, and I hope to inspire you to do the same.

Here's My Proposal to You

Read this book and work through the exercises.

They will help you tremendously to get off to a great start. Some of my actor friends with years of experience have read this book. They said they learned a thing or two and said they wish they had had access to information like this at the beginning of their careers. If they had, they believe they would have had a much easier time and would have been able to avoid some of the pitfalls and save a lot of time. That let me know that this book is exactly what new actors need. It is the base. The fundament. It's information, the method we all can benefit from at the beginning of our careers.

What This Book Can Do for You

The pages of this book contain valuable content for you to use. It's about valid, helpful information by an actor for other actors and artists in general who want more out of their careers and their lives, artists who want to feel more in control of their destiny and who, between jobs, just want to focus on what it is they really want to do. My goal is to make you understand that things can be better than they are, whether they are currently great or terrible! I wrote this book to help you clarify what you want and to give you a methodology that will help you get it.

It will also help answer some of the questions that many of us have:

- How do successful actors get continuous work and make a living doing what they love?

- How can we clarify what it is we want, not only out of life, but also out of our acting careers, what we expect from this industry?

- There are so many things to do. How can we effectively manage our time, set up a plan, and execute that plan to get what we want?

- Actors are freelance professionals, but what if we don't know anything about business? What if we're not business savvy? What do we do?

- I would like to have a friend sit down and tell me what she/he does day by day to conduct the business of being an actor. Who do I know? Who will do that for me?

- How many different ways are there to promote oneself in the industry?

- How can we keep up the drive and create strong motivation to do all the daily tasks necessary to "work the beat" (and land the jobs we want)?

- How do we make that quantum leap into our dream world?

Consider going someplace where you will not be disturbed. Take out a pen and a notepad, read, take notes, answer the questions, and do the exercises in this book. There are not many things in this world that will provide you a quick fix, and this book is not one of them. Things worth having are worth working for. Bernard Hiller, one of my acting teachers and a Hollywood acting coach, once asked us how far we are willing to go to become an artist. I encourage you to ask yourself the same question and, more importantly, to give yourself an honest answer. If you are willing to work hard and go the distance, then you will seriously consider what I have to say between this book's front and back cover.

You will go through the four key factors—clarifying what you want, creating the necessary motivation, planning in detail for *your* success and what you are striving for as an actor, and beginning to adapt twenty-one business concepts to model your career—all of which will give you greater clarity about how your chosen craft fits into your overall scheme of things. The clearer the answer to that question is for you, the stronger your guiding light and the more motivated you will be to go after what you want. When you finish the book, you will have a personalized plan and you will have taken that important first step to getting the results you really want. This is what successful people do.

When you finish going through the first four sections of the book and working on your own personal plan, you can then read Section 5, which is about what I did over a three-month period in New York as an actor. I take you through my daily activities, how I set up office, how I built relationships, and how I kept in contact with industry professionals. You'll see how I monitored my business, my results, how I measured them, the statistics, and more. It's the story you rarely ever get. It is meant to inspire new ways of managing your business as an actor. It's all the information you want to hear from the busy actor on the run.

Guaranteeing Your Success

Can I guarantee that you will be successful if you do all the things I suggest? No. I don't know how motivated you are, how dedicated you are, or how much you will apply yourself. What I can guarantee, however, is that if you follow what I prescribe, you will begin to achieve important results in your life in general. More specifically, the book will help you stay focused on how to improve in your profession and on how you can increase your chances of getting steady work in your chosen field.

Life is passing you by, and if you are not achieving the results you want in your acting career or in any other area of your life, you have three choices: (1) You can put this book down and tell yourself you'll "read it later"; (2) read it and say to yourself, "That was interesting," and leave it at that; or (3) you can take action, take control, and aggressively and systematically go after whatever it is you want. If you choose the latter and put yourself in the right frame of mind, this book will help you fulfill your dreams. You will discover a whole new world, a world you previously did not know.

I wish you good luck on your journey.

Anthony Smith

SETTING THE STAGE

Just to make sure I was on the right track and to make sure I was in line with reality, I talked to many actors, teachers, casting directors, agents, managers, producers, and directors. I received the confirmation I was looking for from the industry. I asked my acting teacher, Wendy Ward—director of the Ward Studio in New York and who has twenty years experience teaching—to give me an idea of who the people are who come through her program. In order to adequately represent the majority of actors who Wendy sees and teaches, I asked her to comment specifically on the following areas and how the actors typically navigate through them: business skills, marketing, and self-promotion; agents and managers; diligence, discipline, drive, and determination; finances; creativity and networking.

This is what she told me:

> We typically attract actors who sense that something is missing in their acting and realize that they need additional training or actors who are feeling stuck in their careers and need a jump-start from our Career Mentoring Workshop.

The Profile

> While we have a wide array of actors joining our program, the most typical student would be a twenty-one- to twenty-five-year-old who has received a BA in acting from a college program, but once in New York senses that something is missing in his/her work. Frequently, these actors find that the academic approach they have learned is not necessarily leading to compelling results in performance. Or, the student may be a very well trained actor with a strong talent but is getting nowhere in his/her career. Both have come to us looking for a school that will help them become more competitive, through further improvement of their acting skills, as well as through a better understanding of what they must do to take responsibility for their careers.

Another typical student might be a twenty-eight- to forty-year-old beginner who has already had some success in another field, but has always wanted to study acting. Ironically, these students frequently do better in our acting classes and in our career-mentoring workshop for two reasons. First, if they have talent, the Meisner work quickly reveals it and develops that talent to a competitive level with their peers. But perhaps more importantly, these students already know what it is to apply a targeted focus to what they hope to achieve. They display great determination because they feel they have little time to waste. And they have already received affirmation in their professional lives outside of theater that solid commitment and personal discipline will lead to a greater payoff in the end.

Business Skills, Marketing, and Self-Promotion

Generally, the actors I see do not have good business skills at all. Most of the ideas they have about marketing are about twenty years old themselves. They don't seem to realize how glutted the industry is and that, in this marketplace, they must find more innovative approaches to getting seen. Last year, Equity reported that there were more actors coming out of training institutions than ever before and that, at the same time, there were fewer jobs than ever before. In this environment, actors must market themselves in a very different way than in the old days of sending out mass mailings and submissively waiting for a reply.

Unfortunately, most actors we come in contact with have no idea how to market themselves, because this is not taught in the university setting, nor is it usually addressed in private studios here in New York. This is why when I opened the Ward Studio ten years ago I asked Janice Hoffmann to develop our Career Mentoring Program. Janice has been honing this workshop for ten years and while other schools have begun to offer various sorts of business-related classes, I believe our program remains ahead of the pack in addressing what the *real* issues are in sustaining a successful career.

Agents & Managers

We have actors who are working and may have agents or managers. But I notice that even those who have an agent can go a year without a job, sometimes without even being sent out. It is critical that actors understand that while getting an agent is important, they can't sit back on their haunches and hope the agent will do the work for them. They need to be in charge of their careers so that when they do obtain representation, they can make the best use of that relationship.

Many of our actors work in the Off-Off Broadway sector, but I've watched actors waste years continuing to do these little productions or showcases, that quite frankly, few industry people will attend anymore. There is this idea that you need things on your résumé. True, but if the things on your résumé are not in significant venues with significant directors or producers, no one cares. We try to give actors a sense of what they must do to take their work to the next level. But we have to combat a sort of generational delusion among young people that somehow they will just be discovered.

Diligence, Discipline, Drive, Determination

The students who come to us already know that we have exceptionally high standards and so most are diligent or learn how to be diligent in our acting program. We drop people who are not meeting our standards and so those who are left are inspired by not being drawn down by dead weight.

We tend to draw actors who are more driven and determined because they get the sense when they interview with us that that is the way we are and that is what we expect. However, even our best prospects find during their training here that there is always room to ratchet up their determination and understand that they will have to if they want to compete. And in this marketplace, you simply must be better trained than other actors. No longer can you rely on good looks. There will be 100 actors like you at the audition. You have to be not only the best actor but the most diligent.

Actors' Finances

We are always addressing finances with our students. The actors I see live with a romantic idea that they need free time more than money. So they take jobs that leave them open for auditions before agents are even sending them out. In the meantime, they end up wasting most of the day away. They may have flexible jobs at restaurants, bars, or late shifts at law firms. But what we notice is that these same actors frequently don't have enough money to pay for classes, headshots, etc. Many are unable to build up a nest egg for the future when they will need to take time off from their jobs. I advise actors to get real jobs and make and save as much money as they can while they're in training so that, later, money won't get in their way. The notion of the struggling actor is a dangerous image for actors to identify with. They should use CEOs of companies as their role models.

Creativity

Over the years I have seen a huge drop in creativity, and this is a great concern of mine. Fortunately, the Meisner work demands that actors use their imaginations in a very robust way and it gets exercised over and over again. But I find this requirement of the training—a strong and effective use of the imagination—is becoming more and more rare in young actors. I have several theories on why this has happened but suffice to say that creativity seems to be on the decline. Much of what we try to do in the Meisner work and in the Career Mentoring Workshop is to reawaken this skill, which is critical to the craft and the career.

Networking

Generally I don't think actors are good networkers. The best that we see are frequently bartenders or students who work in production because they are around new people all the time and become very good at making conversation and acquiring new friends and acquaintances. I think all actors must learn to become good networkers, as this is a relationship business. It can be as simple as striking up conversations with people in elevators, stores restaurants, etc. New York is a very intimidating city because not everyone is friendly, but in the industry, being friendly, open, and polite is extremely important. I am always amazed when young actors respond without a sense of grace or self-respect—and we find that how people treat their instructors and classmates is a very predictable indication of how they will get along with people in the industry. Lesson 1: don't burn any bridges!

All the things you just read are the many of the reasons why I wrote his book. Enjoy.

KEY FACTOR #1:

Clarity Of Vision:
Figuring Out What You Really Want

*"The Future Belongs To Those Who Believe
In The Beauty Of Their Dreams."*

anonymous

CHAPTER 1

Reviewing My Life in Search of Answers

One evening when I was fifteen, I was standing in the kitchen of our house. We had just finished dinner, and my mother had washed the dishes and left them for me to dry (by hand as we had no dishwasher back then!). Sometimes after she finished washing, she would sit and keep me company while I finished the kitchen chores. That evening, while I finished up the dishes and she sat at the table in the kitchen, I stopped, as I did at times, and began to see in front of me an imaginary audience with my mother in the front row. I began speaking aloud, addressing that audience, using words that really made no sense, but that didn't matter to me. What mattered was that in my mind, I had an important message to deliver and my imaginary audience was very interested in what I had to say, because they found the information I was giving them to be of great value. When I finished my brief discourse, I looked at my mother and smiled. She bowed her head as if in prayer, made the sign of the cross, and said to me jokingly, "Boy, I think I did something wrong in raising you, because you ain't right in the head!" I then told her, "Mom, one day you will see that I will be communicating my and other people's messages to large numbers of people. You'll see. One day I will do that. That will be how I make my money!"

I didn't really think much about that in the years to come, at least not consciously. Instead, I got caught in a trap, which had its effect on me realizing my dream.

Becoming a Man

After high school, I didn't really know what I wanted to do, so I joined the air force. The first few days of my basic training changed me forever. The first night, we arrived around 10:00 p.m. in San Antonio, Texas, and were lined up in formation and marched into the barracks. Our sergeant called us into the dayroom. There were forty-eight of us. He said that over the next seven weeks, we would often do things in formation and that he needed volunteers for dorm chief; this person would be in charge of the entire group and four squad leaders, who would each lead a part of the group and report directly to the dorm chief.

He asked for a show of hands of those who felt they would be right for one of those positions. Many raised their hands. Their reasons were different and ranged from "Because I was captain of the football team" to "I've always been a natural leader" to "Because I think I could do the job." I didn't raise my hand, because I didn't want any of those jobs. By the time I had gotten off the plane, I had already decided that I wanted to keep a low profile, get through the train-ing, and move on to my real job. I had been training my body in the few months prior to my departure, so I felt I could withstand any physical test they threw at me. That evening, the sergeant chose the five group leaders, and when we were in formation the next morning, I filed in behind them, as I was not one of the five. So far everything was going according to my plan.

Two days later, I was standing in the mess hall line waiting for my dinner. We did everything in a formation. While waiting in line and before moving forward, we had to stand at attention, take a step, and then be "at ease." At one point there was a mirror, in front of which we had to stand at attention, salute, do an about-face, and then sidestep the rest of the way down the chow line.

One evening, immediately after doing my salute and about-face, I heard, "Airman Smith!"

It was my sergeant, and I immediately jumped to attention and responded with,

"Sir! Yes, sir!"

"Get over here!"

"Sir! Airman Smith reports, sir!"

"Where did you learn how to do that about-face, Airman Smith?"

"I don't know, sir. I taught myself, sir!"

"Good! Tomorrow morning at nine o'clock sharp, I want to see you in my office! Starting tomorrow, you will be the new dorm chief. I'm firing the one we have now."

Trying to disguise my "oh shit" feeling, I promptly responded, "Sir! Yes, sir!" and got back in the chow line.

The next day, I took over for Juroni Thomas as dorm chief. Despite being the third youngest in the group, whose members ranged from eighteen to twenty-seven years of age, I remained the group's leader for the entire seven-week period, and I learned that being in charge wasn't as bad as I originally thought.

I had joined the air force because I wanted to see the world, and that's what I did. I traveled throughout the United States and went to Europe for the first time in my life. I landed in Germany as the ignorant American—I really had no idea where I was. I created a method of learning the language on my own. At the beginning of my stay, there were many times when I should have been working and instead was creating word lists and finding their translations so that I could memorize them. Then came the prepositions and the verbs and their conjugations. That's how I created my base. Within just months, many of my American and German friends envied that I could pick up a language so easily. Within a year, I was considered by many to be fluent, and I was proud of that.

I traveled around Europe and even went to Egypt. Four years after I had enlisted, it was time to make another decision: Do I stay in the military or get out? Well, I still didn't know what I wanted to do with my life. I was twenty-two years old. The only things I knew were that I loved and had a knack for foreign languages and that I loved to travel. That's all. So, I tagged on another two years to my enlistment.

Going to College

I finished my tour back in the States, and after almost six years, I realized that I wanted a military career. After all, it seemed like a good deal. I only had to put in another fourteen years, and then I could retire at around forty, get more than 50 percent of my exit salary each month for the rest of my life, and then start another career. I decided that it would be most beneficial if I became an officer, which meant first going to college. I was tired of seeing young people—officers—come into the military after college, enjoying higher salaries, more power, leadership training, more responsibility, and many other privileges just because they had gone to college. I knew I was capable of doing the same, so at twenty-four, I left the air force and went back to school.

The next big decision was finding a major. I knew I loved language, so I majored in German language and culture, because one day I would return to Europe. One of my minors was Russian, which would help me when I went back to the military, as I wanted to be in intelligence and be a spy. The Russian language intrigued me.

The other reason I chose Russian was for business. I had heard that, economically, Russia would one day open its doors to the West, and I wanted to be there to scoop up some of the money that would come flowing our way. My second minor was, logically enough, business administration.

The college years were some of the most fun of my life. I played football; was one of the team's tricaptains; and was a resident assistant in the dormitory, which meant I had my own room! Lots of friends, great parties, and just livin' life.

Time to Get a Real Job

At age twenty-seven, I graduated from college and went back knocking on the door of the U.S. Air Force. It took me a while, but I finally knew what I wanted to do in life: be an intelligence agent and language specialist, spying in foreign countries and intercepting foreign transmissions for the U.S. government.

When I told the recruiter this, he said that I was a good candidate for this but that I had to first enlist as an officer and that I would have to be available for the first two years to be placed wherever the air force needed me. That meant I could have been responsible for an element of the military police force, fire department, dining hall, officer's club, or whatever! I was stubborn and politely told him that either it would be my way or no way at all. We parted ways, and that was the last I had anything to do with the military.

I then went to work in a printing company, rotating into around-the-clock shifts, placing the pages in a machine that then went down the assembly line to make the magazines. Eight hours a day, placing stacks of pages in a machine, waiting till the stack went down, and then placing other pages in the machine. Eight. Hours. A. Day.

The shift manager was the same age as me, but he was a manager in training and had just graduated from college—just like me! Every time I saw him making his rounds, I asked myself, "What did I do wrong? Why am I using my college education to put stacks of paper in a machine, while he was in management-trainee position?"

Back to School

At age twenty-eight, I made another move that proved to be very significant. After my hopes of returning to the military were shattered and without a clear idea of what I wanted to do with my life, I decided to go back to school and get a masters degree. My university had a foreign exchange program, so I returned to Germany, where I obtained my masters degree in two years. It was another great experience, where I learned more about that country's culture, history, and economic climate. The social life was also great. This was something else I knew I wanted: to be different from the average American and from my friends, who were still at home in the small town in which we grew up.

Within the realm of that experience, I had a chance to reawaken my interest and underdeveloped talent of addressing an audience on the small stage. For two summers I went through a six-week intensive language study at the Millersville University of Pennsylvania, back at the mother school in the United States. Herr and Frau Hens, German nationals and professors, conducted courses for grad students and directed plays as well. All the students were cast in those plays, and I really enjoyed that. I didn't necessarily like every play, but I always enjoyed dressing up and performing on stage.

I graduated when I was twenty-nine and continued working in the part-time job I had begun six months before I graduated. I taught German language and culture lessons to American soldiers. This was another clue for me on my life path: I loved to teach and to aid in other people's learning.

The Sports and Fitness Company

Six months after graduation and while still in Germany, I ran across a news-paper ad that changed the next decade of my life. It was for a position as a tech-nical consultant in the sales and marketing division of Nike's German subsidiary. I would end up working in that company for the next twelve years. In that position, I learned a lot about what really tickled my fancy: sports, pub-lic speaking, teaching, leading people to achieve results, and money.

The first three years in Nike were the second-best time of my adult life. Aside from the numerous talk shows at sporting events that I conducted with world-famous athletes such as Sergei Bubka (world-record pole-vaulter) and Michael Johnson, I spent a week with Michael Jordan, Charles Barkley, Scottie Pippen, David Robinson, where I was an interpreter for them all in press con-ferences as well as their personal escorts during their stays in Germany. I also acted as interpreter for Phil Knight, one of the co-founders of the company, and for Tom Clark, Nike's president at the time.

In addition, I was a model for one of Nike's catalogues and did a radio com-mercial as well. There were also the numerous clinics and presentations about Nike shoe technology that I did for groups of up to 120 people. I went to Moscow on vacation and took a two-week intensive language refresher course, at the end of which I did a clinic at a store that sold Nike shoes on Red Square. These few years were just plain fun!

And then...something changed. I was called into the office of the national sales director for Nike's German subsidiary, who asked if I would be interested in becoming the European sales manager for the Nato bases where Nike sold its products. Ever since I began working for that company, I had been thinking that I wanted a career there. When I was offered this opportunity, I immedi-ately thought about the possibility to grow in a company that had, so far, given me so much.

I thought about the prospect of making more money and about managing people, and I took the job. That's when the fun stopped and things got a lot more serious. I was in the office more and was working longer hours, doing things that I really didn't enjoy. However, I did them anyway and got good results and made money, and I knew that it was an investment in my career. I didn't know exactly what kind of career or where this career would take me, but I knew it was an investment in my future.

After almost two years in that position and having grown the business I had been responsible for managing, I was asked to go to Holland, the headquarters of Nike Europe, to start up the Training & Development Department for the European sales force. This was another significant move for me. Aside from the growth opportunity it provided me, I spent the first three months organizing, planning, and executing a tour of Europe to kick off the training. During a one-month period, we spent two and a half days in each of the eight different European countries; training their sales forces we hit Newcastle in the UK, Milan, Paris, Frankfurt, Barcelona, Stockholm, Amsterdam, and Innsbruck.

That month I was home for a total of one day. I touched home base, washed, dried, and ironed my clothes, and then I was off again. Despite the rigorous travel schedule, it was one of the most rewarding experiences of my professional career. We didn't teach people. We facilitated their learning. We made them think. We stimulated them into taking action. They were inspired by what we did. We made them ponder not only their work, but also their lives. I saw people so moved at the end of the two days that they cried, because they could see the difference we were making in their lives. I knew then that whatever I would go on to do professionally, it must somehow help people improve the quality of their lives.

The Italian Charm

Then, after more than two years and other career opportunities offered to me (which I had refused), I had another decision to make. I had fallen in love with a beautiful Italian girl from a small town near Venice. Over the course of two years, we spent a lot of money traveling back and forth every two weeks on the one-and-a-half-hour flight between Amsterdam and Venice. While I was still working in Holland, we got married and had a son. She wasn't very happy there and neither was I. She wanted out of that country, and I wanted to go back home to the good old United States of America. I'm a sucker for love and sweetness, so I told her that I would take her back home to Italy. When she asked me how I thought I'd be able to work there, not knowing the language, I told her I would learn it.

I applied the same successful technique I had used to learn German some years before. In addition, I bought a book called *Italian in Three Months,* a self-study course that came with four audiocassettes. I was very diligent about finishing each exercise in the book and listening and following the instructions on every audiotape. It took me four months to finish the entire book and to listen to all the cassettes, but I did it and created a base for myself. For a few months, I followed that up with some lessons once a week and I was pretty much on my way to becoming proficient.

This desire to learn Italian was sparked by an incident that occurred the first time I met my wife's mother. She cooked me a great home-cooked Italian meal, after which I wanted to thank her for her hospitality and tell her how I felt about her daughter. Since at that time I hadn't yet learned the language, my fiancée had to translate for me. When I was about to leave, I told her mother that the next time I came back, I would talk to her myself in her language. She said nothing and smiled politely, but I could see in her eyes that she was skeptical that I would really be able to speak Italian upon my return. That challenge made me want to learn the language even more—and I did! The next time I saw her some months later, I spoke to her in her language. Inside myself when I left, I said, "Yes!"

The Move to Italy

It was a difficult decision to go live in Italy, because at the same time, Nike was offering to induct me into an international management trainee program in the States that I could possibly design myself. However, I thought that if I took my wife and newborn child back there, knowing how much she would probably miss her family and friends and culture, we would be divorced in a year. So, Italy it was!

When I finally got to Italy, I was happy because I had done something good for someone else. This was where my wife wanted to be. She was happy, and her family and friends were happy. I, on the other hand, was miserable. I hated it! The first six months were among the saddest of my life. I wanted to return home, and I felt trapped. I felt as if my son wasn't my son anymore, but was rather "their" son.

Looking back, I perceived that the child was the center of attention, and I was just a bystander. My feelings were exaggerated, and I was playing the victim, because I wasn't very happy being there. I finally stood up one day and reclaimed my son, who I thought had slipped away from me. Nevertheless, I still didn't like it there, and my subconscious took over and built a wall between my wife and me. I began to blame her for the way I felt. The wall got higher and higher until one day I could no longer see over it, and we decided to part.

My friends in Nike's Italian organization gave me the chance to get my foot in the door. They offered me the same job that I had been doing at the European level, with responsibility only for Italy. This meant that I had to train my successor to manage the department at the European level and then go to Italy and report to him. For me that was no problem, because I knew that I would grow and advance my career. It was only a question of time. So, after just six months, I was promoted to manage Nike Italy's footwear business, which was about 65 percent of its total revenues. That was a great school for me as well, as I had a chance to exert my leadership capabilities in the management of that business.

After almost two years of that, I began to crave a change. My level of satisfaction in my job and in my life had begun to diminish. This was not the kind of life that I wanted. I loved the company very much. I had the Nike swoosh on my heart (and still do!). I loved leading a team of people to achieve results. I loved the travel, but I didn't like the job itself very much.

Being Honest With Myself

I began to ask myself, why? It was then that I began to finally confront this problem and to find the answers. I wasn't happy doing that job mainly because I had to lead a team of *sales* people, but I myself wasn't a sales guy. I knew it. While I knew that at that level of senior management, it wasn't absolutely necessary for me to be a "sales guy", but rather to coordinate and lead the efforts of the sales team, it still bothered me, because I didn't always feel that I could lead by example. I felt that in that position, I should be, and wanted to be recognized for that.

I was recognized, though, for certain other things: my people skills and honesty and fairness and teamwork, and my management and leadership skills, for my management of the processes that the company had put in place. I was known as a good communicator and as a very good presenter (which, by the way, was one of the things I really liked about my job).

On the other hand, I know that I was a bit too soft at times and not as hard as I should have been with some of my people. At times I also didn't have as much of a pulse on the market as I felt I should have had. I really didn't network as much as I should have and I didn't particularly like going to dinner and lunch with customers, which in Italy is a big thing. I just didn't feel comfortable doing that particular job, in part, because being in Italy for me, often made me feel like a fish out of water. I didn't "feel" the country or that particular job, and, more importantly, I had not the passion I felt was necessary to *totally* commit to it. Given my love for the company and given the fact that professionalism is one of my own personal core values, I felt it only fair to myself first of all and to the company to begin to proactively investigate a change, either within the company or outside of it. I knew for sure that I didn't want to continue on that same career path in sales. Looking back, I'm sure I would have enjoyed marketing a lot more and maybe I would have even been better suited for work in that division, given my creative skills and ambitions.

All things aside, I was a company man. I was responsible, reliable, and trustworthy, and I had good leadership and management skills. Nine times out of ten I got the results my superiors asked for, and I was a good communicator and knew how to get my point across diplomatically. I also had Pan-European experience and I was honest and always had the company's best interests at heart.

Magical Things Happen

To my surprise, I was promoted to national sales manager, where I was to manage all three major divisions—footwear, apparel, and accessories—plus all the support positions. Many congratulated me. It was a challenge, and I was energized to accept it! I was pleased and happy and honored that the company trusted me that much to give me such a large responsibility. I had a renewed sense of energy and enthusiasm for my job. That promotion was the first of three, what I call, magical things that happened during that period of my life.

The second and third magical things that happened had to do with two people I met. The first person was someone I met at our "change of command" ceremony, the moment when I officially took over as sales director. We had organized a gala evening with our top one hundred customers in Italy and invited Fiorello, a famous television personality, to emcee the event. There were presentations that evening by the general manager, the outgoing sales manager, and me. The evening was a great success, and I was riding high on my most recent career success: my promotion. My presentation that night was just the icing on the cake. On stage in front of all those people, I was in my element and I loved it!

The next day, I received a phone call from Fiorello. He asked if I could meet him in Rome, because he was so taken by the event, by my presentation in particular and the enthusiasm that we Nike people conveyed, as well as by the products, that he was seriously thinking of opening a Nike-only store in his hometown. I jumped at the occasion, not only for more business, but also to get to know a person who was doing something that I was very interested in as a profession.

I met with him, his fiancé and his sister. We all hit it off immediately. We all exchanged phone numbers and kept in touch. Fiorello's career was very hot at the time, and he was the number-one television personality in Italy. He was on a six-stop tour as emcee of a famous musical event that was done in the squares of major cities around the country, where some of the most famous musical groups from around the world were invited to play. The events were all televised.

He and his agent invited me to travel with him his entourage and to participate in the events in an exclusive backstage role. I moved when they moved, went to rehearsals with them, ate with them, and basically shadowed their moves. He introduced me to some of the celebrities and artists with whom he worked. I got to learn some of the intricacies of television. It was great, because I had the chance to see firsthand what show business was like.

Fiorello and I developed a friendly relationship where we kept in touch from time to time, and my son and I even spent a weekend at his house with him and his fiancé. The whole experience of meeting him and his family and spending time with him professionally and really seeing what he does behind the scenes brought me closer to a reality that I wanted to experience more of.

Meeting My Angel

The second important meeting during this period occurred when I went to Amsterdam for a couple of days for work, as I did regularly. Upon my return, I boarded a plane for Bologna. I had been running late, and together with a colleague, ran to get on the plane. When we boarded, the other passengers were already seated and waiting for us. My seat was in the second row, right as I entered the plane. The bins above the seats were all full, so I had trouble finding a place to put my computer. I glanced at my seat and saw that the person sitting next to me was a strikingly beautiful young Middle Eastern woman.

Finding a woman like that seated next to me had happened only a few times in all my travels over the last twenty-five years! This gave me incentive to find a place for my computer as quickly as possible. As I put a newspaper on my seat, she said she could put my computer under the seat in front of her. I told her that it would cramp her for the two-hour trip but thanked her anyway. She raised her voice and insisted. Again I politely refused her offer. Then, finally, the flight attendant helped make room in one of the overhead compartments, and the problem was solved.

When I sat down, a great conversation began between this mysterious and beautiful woman and me. We talked about a lot of things. She told me that she came from a large family, that she was an equestrian who had six horses, and had financing from some really important people. I thought to myself, "Hmmm. She sounds like someone pretty important." She proceeded to tell me that she competes internationally, representing her country.

Time flew, and before we knew it, we were in Bologna. The Marconi Airport in Bologna is typical of many Italian airports in that it is small, and passengers must be transported from the aircraft to the terminal in buses. When we got on the bus, she suggested, as I would have if she hadn't beaten me to the punch, that we keep in touch. We exchanged business cards. When I looked at her card, I couldn't believe what I read. I looked at her and said, "Why didn't you tell me?" She replied, "What was I supposed to say? 'Hello, my name is _____ and I'm a princess?'" I prefer not to mention her name or the country where she is from, but she is a genuine princess.

For the following five weeks, we kept in touch regularly. Like two teenagers, we sent text messages back and forth five to six times each day, and at times we had long telephone conversations. We had become instant friends. Unfortunately, we didn't see each other much during those five weeks, but our relationship was intense nevertheless and purely platonic. She was an incredible source of inspiration and encouragement for me. I had told her about my desire to one day follow my dreams, and she told me that I had to do it soon, as time will only pass me by.

At the end of those five weeks, she gave me a book called *The Alchemist* and told me she hoped the book would "inspire me to take action and do what I knew I had to do." She then left Italy and practically disappeared from my life. I missed her. I missed her messages, her words, her voice, her friendship, her understanding, her encouragement, her inspiration. She was one of the few people who seemed to understand me. She was like an angel, who appeared in my life to give me a message and then disappeared. I will never forget her.

I Knew It Was Time

These three significant events—my promotion, meeting Fiorello, and meeting the princess—all led me to believe that life had given me messages and that it was time to make a decision.

Shortly after "the vanishing" of the princess, which was approximately six months after my promotion to national sales manager, I began to feel the same way I had before my promotion: tired, unhappy, unmotivated, and I lacked drive. I knew that if my career continued to go in the sales direction, I wouldn't be very happy, despite being able to become very well off financially.

The only other job that I wanted in Nike Italy was that of general manager (GM). That didn't seem likely in the near future, as the GM at the time was on his way out and another was about to replace him, which meant that I wouldn't get a chance at the position for another three or four years. I felt my only alternative to further my career, at least to have a chance to do something I liked, was to leave the country and get transferred to Holland or back to the States. But that wasn't an alternative, because I didn't want to be away from my four-year-old son.

This was the same period during which my marriage had finally gone tilt to the point that a decision had to be made. So I moved out of the house, which marked the beginning of my new life.

Conversation with the Man in the Mirror

One day during that same period, I got up on a Monday morning, walked into the bathroom. While washing my hands, I stopped to look at myself in the mirror. I scanned my head, my hair, my teeth, nose, cheeks, lips, forehead, eyebrows, ears, and eyes. I looked deep into my eyes and asked myself a question that would change the course of my life: "Why are you going into the office today?"

The answers I gave myself were obvious, standard, and very logical. I told myself that it was necessary to continue on this road, because I had a family to maintain, I had a son to take care of, I had to think about my future, the company loves me, it's a great company, I had great career opportunities, I could retire a millionaire…

All these things I mentioned were true, but I kept asking questions. Soon this question-and-answer session turned into a conversation between the man in the mirror (him) and me:

Him: Are you happy, Tony? I mean, are you really happy?

Me: No.

Him: Why not?

Me: I don't know. I'm not really into my job. I'm not enjoying it.

Him: Why not? What is it that you don't like about it?

Me: Let me just say that I think my talent could be better used in another division in which I could use my creativity, like in marketing for example. It would be more fun. I'm not having fun anymore. I'm not enjoying my work. I love the company, but not the job.

Him: And what is it that you like about your job?

Me: I had fun when I was an EKIN (technical consultant), conducting training courses and interviews and speaking in public. In fact, even though I love this company and what it stands for, the only other thing I really love about my job is that I have to present from time to time. I love that!

I also really like managing people, motivating them, giving them feedback, helping them improve and develop themselves. I love the coaching sessions when I can look someone in the eye and tell them how they are doing in their job. I love writing up the evaluations on people. I love talking to people about what their career opportunities could be, about what it is they want, about the future, the comparison between the way they see themselves in their jobs and the way I see them.

I like going to the European HQ to the meetings and interacting with my colleagues, who have the same responsibility as I do in the different countries. I like traveling. I always look forward to the big sales meetings, because it is a chance to travel, mingle with other Europeans, give presentations. I love presenting and giving speeches! I like the possibilities this company offers to grow and develop oneself and to make money; I like the stock options, bonuses, and pay raises.

I like the human side of the business. I like dealing with people, not managing sales and numbers and reaching targets and talking to customers about discounts and margins and retail presentation.

Him: So what do you want to do?

Me: I don't know.

Him: "I don't know" is not an acceptable answer! What do you want to do?

Me: I'm going into the office today!

Him: What do you like, Tony? Whatever you end up doing in the future, what elements, things, activities would you like to include?

Me: Well, I like presenting, acting, sports, women, and money.

Him: Women? Money? What does that mean?

Me: It means that whatever I do, I would like to work around women and men. I can't imagine a profession in which I don't see any women. Doesn't mean I have to sleep with all of them, but I love admiring them, having them around, talking to them. That's all. As for the money, I want to make a comfortable living so that I don't have to worry about whether the government will give me a pension or not. I want to live a good life.

Him: I know that! What would you like to *do* instead? What about sports? Would you like to be a professional athlete?

Me: I would liked to have been, but I didn't believe enough in myself and now it's a little late.

Him: Let me ask you this, Tony: If you could do *anything* you wanted in life, no limits, what would you do?

Me: I'd like to be an actor or have my own television program back in the States. I'd like to have my own corporation with different divisions: me as an actor, television host, seminar leader, keynote speaker. A portion of all proceeds would go to charity. This would all happen under the umbrella of innovation, because everything I did would be different than most things one finds in the marketplace today.

Him: You want to be an actor, huh?

Me: Yes.

Him: I've heard this from you before. You said this some years ago. Why didn't you go for it before?

Me: That's a good question. I guess I got caught up in the money and the career, and kind of lost sight of what I really wanted.

Him: And now you want to be an actor?
Me: Yeah! That's what I would really like to do. It must be the coolest profession in the world. It's not about the fame and the glory; it's about finally doing something I really love.

Him: You realize that, at forty years of age, it will not be the easiest thing to do? You realize that most people in that profession start at a very early age, and by the time they are your age, they have solid experience?

Me: Yes, but you asked me if I could do anything I wanted, what would it be. That's my answer.

Him: And then I asked you what you are going to do. So here's the thing, Tony. You are not happy with your current job. You love the company, but you don't like the job. You could have other opportunities within the company, but they would probably take you outside the country. You don't want to do that, because of your son being here. You have two alternatives. You can either stay here and be unhappy, or you can do something about your situation.

Do you really want to be an actor and speaker and television host, or will it remain just a dream? If you decide not to act upon your wishes and dreams and stay here where you are, just know that one day you could wake up and wish you had done something about it. You just might regret that you lacked the courage to confront what's inside you now, and you will never know how things might have turned out.

(Pause)

Him: Well?

Me: I want to go for what I want.

Him: With that conviction? If that's all the passion you can muster up, then you need to stay where you are, because you'll never go anywhere. Let me ask you again: What do you want to do?

Me: I want to go for what I want!

Him: Okay! Are you sure?

Me: Yes! Why do you keep asking me the same question?

Him: Because, first of all, you need to realize that it might not be easy. Second, if you don't have the discipline and the motivation deep down to stick with it, then it won't happen. And third, if you change your mind and decide to stay here and continue to do what you're doing, then keep your fucking mouth shut about dreams and wishes and don't complain. Just keep on humpin' till you retire! Got it? And if in the future you want to talk about it again, don't talk to me, because I'm sick of hearing it! Either you do something about it or shut the fuck up!

Me: I'm gonna do it!

Him: Okay! Now, what needs to happen for you to begin going after what you want?

Me: I need to go and study.

Him: Good. You can take some evening courses.

Me: No! I'll be too tired after work. I want to take some time off work and dedicate myself to it full-time.

Him: Okay. How much time off?

Me: At least a year?

Him: Be more specific. Twelve months, eighteen months? How much time?

Me: A year and a half. Eighteen months. But I need to figure it all out and decide what my plan is; then I'll know for sure. I'll start working on that this week. By next weekend I'll have a plan worked out, and I will know how much time off I need, what I will do, and how much money I will need during that time period.

Him: Do you think you will be ready to take off work, quit Nike this year?

Me: No, unfortunately not, considering my obligations—my living expenses, my schooling, and travel—I will need at least $60,000 and I don't have that much money lying around that I can spend right now. And besides, I have responsibilities.

Him: So when do you think you will have that money and be able to take off work?

Me: If I stay at Nike and if everything goes well—stock options mature, I get good evaluations, and my pay raises—five years.

Him: That's too long! You're already forty years old! If you wait until you're forty-five, that's a little late. Don't you think?

Me: You're right. I need to shorten that time period. I need to figure out where I'm going to get that much money faster.

The Decision

The conversation ended that way and my decision was made. I had to find a way to get my hands on some more money, quickly. And one thing was clear. To get it, I was going to have to think outside the box.

As I tried to figure things out, map out my plan, clarify my objectives, and figure out how to get the money, more than a year had passed and my desire to achieve my newly defined goal was as intense as it had ever been. I was ready!

Just at that time, an opportunity arose that I had to investigate. An executive search agency called me for an interview. One of their customers was a large multinational company, a worldwide leader in its industry, and was looking for a country manager for Italy. At least on paper I seemed to fit the profile, so they asked if I was available for an interview.

It is usually very interesting to go on these interviews, even if you're not looking for a job, because you find out about the market and you learn your worth. In this interview, I found out that the client I was interviewing for was Levi Strauss Italy. One thing led to another, and eight interviews, two trips to Brussels, a psychological and management profile test, and two offers later, I was on my way to getting the money I needed to fund my project.

Strategic Moves and Conversation with Nike's President

I had the pleasure of personally saying good-bye to Charlie Denson, one of the then co presidents of the company. I have a tremendous amount of respect for him. He was with another person I hold in very high esteem—Gary De Stefano, who was on a trip to Turin, Italy, for a senior management meeting. Since I didn't feel it was right for me to be involved in that meeting, I bowed out gracefully, but I did later meet with them to say farewell personally.

Charlie asked me why, after twelve years, I decided to leave the company. I answered, "I'm leaving because of something you taught me." He asked what that was. I said, "One day I was working on the strategic plan for Italy sales. As always, I thought about our situation in the market today. I analyzed the competition and where we would like to be in one, three, five years from now, how we would like to be perceived in the marketplace, who our end consumers will be, what the face of retail will look like, the customers we will serve, and how we will serve them. I thought about all the things that need to happen in order for our plans to come alive and actually happen, the key factors for success. I had to think about how all those things fit into the global and European strategies. I had to take a hard look at the resources I had to work with and decide how to best utilize them to reach our objectives. There had to be a precise plan mapped out, and there had to be a monitoring mechanism in place to ensure that the plan would actually be executed.

I've done this many times over the years and I asked myself, 'If I applied this same process to my life and my goals and what I want to achieve, and if I spent this much time doing it, I wonder what would come of it?' So, I erased all the Nike information from the strategic plan on my computer, and I entered my personal information.

Now I know precisely what my goal is. I know where I want to be in five years. I know what needs to happen in order for me to get there. I know what my key factors for success are. I know what resources I have that will help me get there and how I can best utilize them. I have a monitoring mechanism in place and a budget. I know how much money it will take and how much I have to invest. I took the process I learned from you and applied it to my life. I have to at least try this, Charlie. If I don't, I'll always be wondering what would have happened if…And I don't want to be in that position."

Another thing that is very important, and that I already had, is the attitude that anything is possible and that I should "Accept No Limits" (a previous company slogan). If I really want something, I should "Just Do It."

I told Charlie that I might be back one day and that I hoped I would be welcome with open arms. I assured him my reason for leaving had nothing to do with my like or dislike for the company, because I loved the company. I was leaving because there was something very strong inside of me saying that I had to do this!

A Necessary Step in the Plan

The move to Levi's was necessary to achieve my goal in a shorter amount of time. When you grow up in a company, you can make good money, but it's said that ambitious individuals on a career and money-making path should change companies every seven years because it allows them to achieve two things: personal/professional growth and quick financial advancement.

I stayed true to my values, especially that of professionalism, but when I went to work for Levi's, it wasn't for my love of jeans. I gave them all the professionalism I could and helped that company achieve the results they hired me to get. I went there because I was on a mission to utilize the resources I had at my disposal—my experience—to get the money I needed to fund my project. I had to think outside the box, which for me meant changing companies, because it is a chance to get a substantial increase in salary. I would stay there only as long as necessary to achieve that part of my goal and to prepare the road for my successor in the most professional way possible; then I would move on to the next phase of my project.

After a year of having gotten to know my new company better, I had begun to see that there was a difference between, what they hired me to do and what I was actually asked to do. Further, I didn't like the company. To be honest, it was kind of tough to get used to after my previously positive corporate experience and living a great company culture. I disagreed with the strategies, which I felt were very shortsighted and just plain wrong for the Italian market. I couldn't stand behind them. So I told my boss how I felt about everything. He smiled and said that I was right but that the company was so big that the changes I suggested would take time to sell internally and to put in place.

Immediately I thought about my goal and realized that it was not to save this company and to sacrifice my time, effort, and energy to try making a difference there. I thanked him for his answer and his candor and politely told him that I would stay long enough for them to find a successor and to prepare the group for the change of command, and then I would leave. After all, I had already achieved my initial goal: to get additional experience and money to fund my project. So, I continued on to the next phase of my strategy. I left knowing though that I was as professional as I could be. I gave it my all to help the company reach its goals and I feel good about that.

Since then, I have been on this mission to reach my own personal goals. I'm happy to say that I am well on my way. I'm stopping the story here, even though there is much more to tell. The objective of this first part of the book is to examine the lessons I learned along the way, and writing and examining my story have been very valuable, helping me clarify what it is I really want in life. Now that you have seen how I did it, look at the following lessons I learned, and try to do the same thing.

CHAPTER 2

The Lessons I Learned

It's always easier in hindsight to see what we did right or wrong or what we could have done better. Some say that life will repeatedly present you with certain messages and challenges until you are able to resolve them. I believe that. The reason I included this section in the book is not to simply share with you what I've learned about myself, but rather so you can do the same thing after seeing how I did it. There is no quick fix. It is a process.

When was the last time you spent a couple of hours just thinking about yourself? About your life and where you've been and where you're going? This exercise is for all those people who say, "I don't know" when you ask them, "What profession would you like to have?" Spending this time will help you have more clarity about who you are, what you stand for, the things you want to pursue, and the resources you already have to help you get there.

The following things are what I learned about myself over the years, and there is certainly more to tell than what is listed. What I discovered while writing my life story and reflecting on the past and how I got to where I am now has helped me gain greater clarity and the drive to reach my dreams. I am revealing myself and my process to you to make a point, and to show you how to do it for yourself. The following are just twenty-two of the many lessons I learned from my past.

My Personal Lesson #1: Values

I learned a lot about myself over the last twenty years, including what I stand for: honesty, integrity, empathy, fairness, energy, conviction, determination, method, creativity, courage, credibility, professionalism, and preparation. I realized that these are the principles that have guided me over the years; the principles that define who I am as a person and that I like being associated with.

What I Learned

I want to leave a legacy. These are the things I want included in my life. I have identified with these values, and I want them to guide me. They have shown me the way to tranquility, peace of mind, and success, and I will take them with me on my journey, as I know they will help me along the way.

My Personal Lesson # 2: Family

My family isn't close. I had a normal, average childhood with no major defining moments. I have two older brothers and a younger sister. Only my sister has remained in our hometown. Over the years, I've made efforts to keep in touch every few months with my siblings, but they weren't very responsive. Therefore, I cut back on contacting them, and over the last two decades, we've talked only a couple of times a year. We got together every couple of years, and we would all visit our parents at least once a year, but often at different times. Only recently have we begun to have more contact, which comes from efforts on both sides.

I felt sad for my parents and could imagine it was not a great thing to have your kids spread out all over the world.

What I Learned

For the longest time I blamed my siblings for their behavior, but I realize that I am also to blame. It is rarely one side's fault, but rather a combination of reasons contributes to things turning out as they do. I have a choice to either do something about this relationship, to improve it, or continue to let it stagnate. My parents are my parents, and after all they have done for us, they deserve our support. Anyway, I realized that once I thought about it, a decision to continue doing nothing is in itself a decision.

My Personal Lesson #3: Determination

This is a trait that I learned I have deep inside me. I have repeatedly been able to achieve my objectives in part because of the drive, desire, and determination to persist until I reach my goal. I truly believe that at least 50 percent of one's mental attitude affects the outcome of any given process to reach an objective.

When I first started working many years ago, I noticed that my boss drove a BMW. I told a colleague that one day I would be in a position that would allow me to drive a BMW, too. I told him that it would be the consequence of the job I had, which is really what I strived for. A year and a half later, I had a company car that was a BMW 5 series, because I had reached my goal of becoming a midlevel manager.

Other examples of determination include my desire to learn German and Italian and how I did it on my own. I learned German by first folding a piece of paper lengthwise so there were four columns. I filled up the first and third columns on the front and back with every basic word I thought I would need and its opposite (if there was one), such as fast/slow, good/bad, and so on. Then I filled up the second and fourth columns with the German translations of those words that I either got by looking them up in a dictionary or by asking someone.

I carried that list around with me and studied it religiously in every spare moment I had: while waiting in line at the supermarket, when I got stuck in traffic, at home, on the pot, whatever! I did that until I memorized the entire list, and then I created another one. I listed all the simple verbs, such as *to have*, *to go*, *to be*, *to want*, and so on, and their conjugations. The prepositions were part of the other list, and in this way I was able to create a base of conversation.

When I interacted with someone German—a friend, a store clerk, or whoever—I always insisted on speaking German. When I first started learning the language, people didn't always have much patience and wanted to speak English if they could and if it was better than my German. I spoke German; they replied in English. I spoke German again. They showed their impatience and responded in English. I insisted and continued to speak German until they broke. I won, and that's how I kept in practice. I used every opportunity to learn and get better.

In addition, to help my pronunciation, every morning I read one sentence aloud out of a German newspaper at least twenty-five times. Usually, the first time reading the sentence was difficult, and I stammered and the reading was slow. By the twenty-fifth time, I was reading it like a German. Well, almost. My motivation? I was twenty years old and wanted to talk to the German girls!

One night I went to a club with my buddy Roland. He couldn't speak German. We were standing at the bar, and he saw a nice girl he wanted to meet. He asked if I would go talk to her and tell her that he wanted to meet her. I went over and talked to the girl, and the two of us hit it off. I ended up with the girl, and he was upset. I've talked about how my values include honesty and fairness. As you can see, these were two values that I developed a few years later.

In learning Italian I did the same thing, except I added the book program and four audiocassettes to my study technique. I went through the entire book. Aside from doing every exercise on every page, I also listened to every cassette numerous times while driving. I repeated after the people on the tape, while people drove by and looked at me as if I were crazy. I just waved or smiled and kept on keepin' on! Remember my motivation? Part of it was the challenge in my future mother-in-law's eyes. Part of it was I knew that if I was going to work in Italy at a high level, it was absolutely necessary that I speak proficiently.

What I Learned

I must always remember that determination is one of the things that has enabled me to achieve my goals all throughout my life. It is a gift I have, and the more I am driven by it, the more I can overcome odds that most people consider impossible. This is one of my key factors for success, and I must never forget how much it pays off in the end.

My Personal Lesson #4: The Enjoyment Derived from Doing for Others

I realized how much I enjoy doing things for other people—to help, counsel, and give advice. It gives me a feeling of satisfaction. When I'm helping people, I feel in my element, such as when I had to coach and counsel people during my Nike days; or back in my military days when I had to give advice and train new people coming into the group; and later as a teacher counseling U.S. soldiers on different aspects of German culture. I often found myself in situations of leadership where coaching was important and people looked at me for guidance. In these situations, I felt "in my element."

What I Learned

Whatever I decide to do in my life, it must include helping people improve the quality of their lives. I derive great satisfaction from that, and I want it to always be a part of who I am. I want my son and those whose lives I touch to remember me in that way.

My Personal Lesson #5: No Confrontation

I learned that I'm not one for confrontation. I preferred to avoid it, sometimes at all costs. For me it was more important to find a pacific solution rather than argue. I didn't want to risk being wrong and having to defend my position. It was more important to just avoid the confrontation altogether. Many times I lost out. Sometimes I even lost face. It's not a good feeling, and I don't want it to happen again.

What I Learned

After reflecting on this, I realized that sometimes I was simply afraid of the negative answer I might receive or of what someone might say. It was ridiculous. They were just words. It made no sense.

Once again, I must follow my instincts and stand up for what I believe in. I must express myself completely. Don't hold back! Besides, it will help me in my acting! Like Bernard Hiller, a Hollywood acting coach once told me, "You never know how far you can go until you go as far as you can go."

My Personal Lesson #6: I'm Not the Sales Guy!

One of the most important things I learned was that sales and sales management were the furthest things from my heart. I enjoyed the money, the prestige, the people management, and the leadership skills that were necessary to lead a team of salespeople. But talking sales, margins, number crunching, discounts, retail calculations and math, talking with customers, and going to dinner with them were all things I didn't want to do. I didn't feel in my element, and I didn't feel as though I could always lead by example, because I didn't begin early in my career as a salesperson. Some of that certainly had to do with my beliefs. I did have the skill set to be a sales manager, but I just didn't like it. That's not to say the company wasn't right for me or that I couldn't have contributed in a different way. I love that company even today. I just think that I could have done better and been happier had I gone into marketing or into a position where I could have used my creativity a lot more.

What I Learned

I always desired showing people how to do something by my example. Think about what I am good at, what I am passionate about, what I strongly believe in and make that the example. The money and the power and prestige and even the career opportunities are not the only things that contribute to my happiness. A professor of mine once told me to study what I was passionate about, excel at it, and the money will come.

My Personal Lesson #7: Doing Things for the Wrong Reasons

The whole sales management thing made me realize how important it is to do things you are really passionate about—and not because of what it will bring you. That's the lesson I learned from three instances in my life in which I followed the wrong path. The first was in college. There was a moment during my freshman or sophomore year when I had the choice to play either receiver or defensive back on the football team. I chose receiver because of the glory I could have from making catches and scoring.

The second instance was when I went into sales instead of marketing, where I could have used my creativity and where I probably would have had much more fun. At the time, I thought about how much more money I could make working in sales.

The third instance was when I had the chance to return to the States but decided to move to Italy. I had been thinking about how bad things could be if I went to the States.

The point is, I realized how many times in my life I didn't follow my instinct and my desire. I always had a reason why I should do the opposite of my gut instinct and desire. One thing is for sure: I can't turn back the clock, nor do I want to. I want to go forward and I will. I would not be the person I am had I traveled a different road.

What I Learned

I must follow my heart. Life is passing me by, and the longer I wait to do what I want, the more opportunities I will miss. Just do it!

My Personal Lesson #8: Creativity and the Desire to Be Different

I joined the air force because I wanted to be different and to see the world. I studied German and Russian partly because I liked the idea of speaking a foreign language and living and functioning in another country.

I have become known for giving presentations that are different and innovative.

I worked many years for a company that was and still is very innovative. I never liked wearing name-brand clothing. I never liked following trends.

I love being creative. I love the word *innovation*, using my imagination, trying to come up with new ways to do things. I love the question "How many different ways are there to get what you want?" (You'll repeatedly see that question in this book.) I love setting myself apart from the masses. I never liked being in the status quo. I never liked being one of the pack, doing the same things as everyone else.

What I Learned

Nike taught me that those who risk being different are often the ones who reap the greatest rewards. I desire to be a trendsetter, not a follower. Especially in acting, TV hosting, and industrials work (as in corporate acting jobs, spokesperson, or corporate videos), if I don't set myself apart from the other actors and speakers, I will just be another number. I must continuously think of new ways to promote myself and have fun doing it!

My Personal Lesson #9: My Secrets

I had a lot of secrets, things I didn't want to tell anyone, things I was afraid to reveal about myself for fear of shame. Oftentimes it was for no reason except to protect my privacy and because of insecurity. I have carried this way of thinking with me over the years. Only when I started to ask myself why, did I start to get answers. I found that I was wasting a lot of valuable energy by holding things in and keeping them secret. We'll talk about that later.

What I Learned

Letting things go and getting rid of old baggage can be very liberating. It helps release valuable energy that I can then use in other, more creative ways. Be conscious of what it is I'm holding back and let it out.

My Personal Lesson #10: Emotions

As a result of my childhood and the way I was raised, I often held things in. I began noticing that I wasn't very expressive when in conversations in private and with friends. I used to get punished severely when I was young and then was told not to cry. When I was playing football, we would sometimes have to take a hit, but "real men" never cried. In the military it was the same. You just didn't cry. Consequently, I have a tendency to maintain a stone mask as if I have everything under control, when in fact it is not always that way.

When I am on stage presenting, however, it is a different story. I was and still am very expressive. This is something I noticed about myself and that others noticed and sometimes told me. In acting, on the other hand, I would like to pull out deeper emotions that I have difficulty accessing. I'm making progress, but it will take time.

What I Learned

Be conscious of my behavior and of what I'm holding back. Be equally as conscious of what it is I want to express. I tell myself it's okay to cry and that it doesn't mean I'm soft or not a real man. As I said in the previous section, let it out!

My Personal Lesson #11: Time Alone

One of the things I realized about myself is that I like spending time alone. I enjoy coming home and not having anyone to deal with. Yes, it is lonely at times, and, yes, I worried about ending up alone, but over the last several years, I enjoyed this time of solitude.

What I Learned

Time with myself helps me disconnect from the rest of the world, to relax, think, meditate. Like all things, it must be balanced. If I need that and it makes me feel good, then I must make sure I have it.

My Personal Lesson #12: The Kinds of Women I Attract

Without going into great detail here, I've pondered the kinds of women I have attracted over the years. They say there is a reason why we attract certain people and steer away from others. I began noticing certain things that my women over the years had in common: they were extremely sweet, very responsible, and generous; they looked up to me and were "nice girls"; in other words, they were not promiscuous and were somewhat conservative and traditional, but not so adventurous.

I also realized that I've always been the one to end my relationships. I ask myself why.

What I Learned

Aside from the meaningful relationships I ended in the past, I'm now divorced from a good woman. It was certainly more my fault than hers. I must come to terms with why I am always the one to run away from my lovers. I can choose to find out or leave it be, but before I tie another knot, I need to find out.

My Personal Lesson #13: My Biggest Successes over the Years

- Becoming a father
- Earning a bachelor's degree
- Earning a master's degree (having studied German at a German university)
- Career at Nike

- Learned Italian fluently
- Learned German fluently
- Studied Russian and gave a presentation in Russian to a group on Red Square
- Deal negotiated with the other company
- Country managing director in Levi's
- Took the step toward realizing my dream
- Founded a company that is doing well and that creates flexibility to do what I want
- Formed an objective idea as to my potential as an actor and a host

What I Learned

There is also a series of smaller successes. I am capable of many things, big things. I must only have the courage to explore and apply my experience to achieve my goals. Reaching goals is about what Bernard Hiller, a Hollywood acting coach, calls the "language of success." I realize that each time I tackle a new challenge, the situation might be different, but the formula to achieve success is the same.

My Personal Lesson #14: My Biggest Disappointments over the Years

I prefer to keep this area private, only because I feel I would have to explain why something was a disappointment and why it happened. Doing that now would defeat the purpose of this section. I will, however, share with you some of the lessons I learned from these disappointments.

What I Learned

Once, when I was younger, I got caught doing something I knew I shouldn't have. However, the people around me knew I had made an error in judgment. They knew that I was basically a good person who went down the wrong path momentarily, so I was forgiven. Immediately. Their forgiveness moved me and taught me that if you possess good will, it can come back to help you when the chips are down.

I also learned from another incident that one foolish moment can ruin a lot of things for you. There were a couple of those moments in my life, and they are perhaps the reason why I am so rational today. I reflect on the consequences of my actions. I must take full responsibility for what I do, because the consequences could be with me forever.

My Personal Lesson #15: Desire to Be a Great Speaker and Teacher

Other than the time when I was fifteen years old and standing in the kitchen talking to my mother and my imaginary audience, there were other instances throughout my childhood where I manifested that same desire to become a great speaker, both while playing and while working. I would often imagine standing in front of a large group of people, giving a performance or speaking.

I naturally gravitated toward speaking opportunities in Nike. I jumped at the chance to do interviews and talk shows with athletes, to interpret for our company founder and president, and to engage in press conferences and interviews for Michael Jordan and other athletes.

I thoroughly enjoyed giving presentations as a technical consultant to large groups of people, and speaking at clinics to smaller groups when I was at Nike. It is exhilarating.

When I became sales manager for the military bases in Europe, I often imagined doing a magnificent presentation for my clients—something I never actually did. It was to be great with music, dancers, lights, sketches, scenography, and the whole nine yards. I used to envision that they would be fantastic. There were times, however, when I did miniature versions of them.

When I was national sales manager, I enjoyed presenting to my sales reps. Oftentimes when we had our sales meetings, there was a lineup of speakers on the first day: the general manager, marketing director, retail merchandising manager, divisional sales manager, information technology manager, and me. My objective was always to ensure that, of all these presentations, mine would be the most remembered. To ensure that happened, I strived to create new ways to present different concepts.

Finally, I often envisioned being invited to give a presentation to the entire Nike sales and marketing family at a world sales meeting. I still dream of doing that one day. It would be like a homecoming.

What I Learned

I have very good communication and public-speaking skills. I am objective about this, even though it might sound as if I am boasting. But the purpose of this section is to show how important it is to recognize your strong and weak points, and to look at what you can learn from looking back in your life. I want to use these skills to reach large groups of people in whatever form I can to spread a good message and to help others improve the quality of their lives.

My Personal Lesson #16: Leadership, Coaching, Teaching

In this area I bloomed gradually. In high school I was not a leader. I was always pretty shy and timid about expressing myself and standing up for what I thought was right. Once I went into the military, I began to see a change in myself that might not have happened had I not ventured out on my own at the age of eighteen.

The first time I was cast into a leadership position was in the first days of my military basic training when I was assigned as group leader. Later on in my military career, I was entrusted with the task of training new people coming into our squadron group. I always tried to do my job well and wanted to be respected for such. I think I was successful at that.

In college I jumped at the chance to become a resident assistant (RA) in the dormitory. At the age of twenty-four, I was older when I began college, so I wanted my own room. Getting an RA position was one way to achieve this, and I got it. Once again I found myself in a leadership role.

I also played football in college and was often called "Grandpa," because I was older than the rest. Nevertheless, I was a starter, and in my senior year I was one of the tri-captains of the team. At the end of my senior year, I was awarded with the first annual senior leadership award, given to the player who demonstrated a high degree of leadership throughout the season. I was flattered and gladly accepted.

Because of my pre-college experiences, my friends and classmates often looked up to me for, what seemed to them, my wisdom and life experience. And I was always open to learning new things. Those young bucks often challenged me and taught me a lot. And I taught them a thing or two as well! For those experiences I am grateful.

Although those were the most significant and memorable leadership experiences as I grew and developed, I realize now that the most important aspect was the ability to lead myself. Even in the leadership courses I facilitate today, I always begin with the self, because if one can't lead himself, how on earth can he lead others?

What I Learned

My leadership ability gives me a competitive advantage, and I want to use it to not only do good things, but also to help me face life's inevitable challenges, which I will approach willingly and unwillingly throughout my life.

I learned a lot about myself as a whole, and now I know what it takes to perform, delegate, develop people, assist the stragglers, give and receive feedback, clarify expectations, give instructions, and supervise. I also learned what it means to earn people's respect through leadership.

My Personal Lesson #17: Indecision

Something else that has repeatedly surfaced in my life is my inability to make swift decisions. I went into the military because I didn't know what I wanted to do. I extended my enlistment, again because I didn't know what I wanted to do. Indecision has followed me through a good part of my life, even in my work. I found that the clearer my goals are, the easier it is to decide things. I also realized that not making a decision is a decision in itself.

What I Learned

Clarify my desires as much as possible. That makes it easier to decide. For everyday decisions, however, this is not always easy. I try and follow Anthony Robbins's advice and practice making decisions each day, being conscious of deciding even the smallest things. It's kind of like auditioning. The more you do it, the more comfortable you feel. I began realizing that anything I do starts first with my decision to do it. It gives me more confidence when I must make the bigger decisions.

My Personal Lesson #18: Foreign Languages

I am proud of the energy and ease with which I attacked learning the German language. Determination certainly helped, but I must recognize that I have a knack for language. I applied the same technique with Italian as I did with German and became fluent very quickly in that language as well. And even though I never reached full proficiency in Russian, it was fun to learn, and I did have the opportunity to give a presentation at a store at a shopping center on Red Square back in 1991.

What I Learned

Language is something I am good at. If nothing else, it adds to my self-confidence. As someone who loves to communicate, this gives me an avenue to reach an even greater number of people. If learning another language could somehow help me in the future, I know I can learn it and use it to help me reach a goal.

My Personal Lesson #19: Strong Clues

In her world-renowned book *The Artist's Way*, Julia Cameron talks about how, when we are clear on what we want in life and are highly motivated to get it, the universe conspires to help us. I agree with her. If we take the time to reflect on our lives, we will see that the universe has given us clues to help us decide, to test our willingness and resolve, to put us on the right path. Getting promoted to national sales manager, meeting Rosario Fiorello, and meeting the princess all helped me to decide where I really wanted to go.

Sometime later, I was tested to see if I really wanted to become an actor or if I wanted to continue develop my company's business. I suddenly had a lot of business coming my way. I ended up turning it into an opportunity to get what I wanted. But that's another story.

I also firmly believe that when you decide you really want something, and I mean with a strong desire that drives you, magical things start to happen around you. For example, you might overhear someone talking and get an idea to help you solve a problem. You might see an ad in the newspaper, hear something on the radio, or see something on television that helps you find a solution you need or reach an objective. Someone might say something in conversation that will spark achieving what you want.

As I will talk about later, when you get into the habit of thinking that every situation, every person you come in contact with gives you something, figure out what that something is and magical things happen.

What I Learned

Keep my eyes and ears open. I train myself constantly in this. I ask myself this question each time I go into and come out of a new situation or conversation, see something on television, attend a class, or see something on the Internet: "How can what I'm experiencing now help me?"

My Personal Lesson #20: You Gravitate Naturally Towards What You Want When You Have Strong Motivation

Having strong motivation for your goals is one of the major lessons I learned in my life. If you are *really* motivated, you will automatically gravitate toward your goals. Decisions on how to get there will become easier. Actions needed to get there will come naturally and be easier to execute. It's like magic.

What I Learned

My experience tells me that when my motivation is strong and I'm crystal clear about what I want, I reach my goals 99 percent of the time. If there is something I want and the motivation isn't quite there, I need to create it. Now I know how to do that.

My Personal Lesson #21: Taking Responsibility for My Own Actions

As a young adult, I began to realize that I am responsible, together with only God, for the results that I get. I refuse to put my destiny in someone else's hands. I don't make someone else responsible for my motivation. If something didn't go the way I wanted it to, I began to ask myself, "What could I have done better?" or "What could I do differently next time so that doesn't happen?" This is the same thing Sergeant Richard told me once when I was just a young buck in the military, and it's something I never forgot. After he told me that, I began to notice all those people who often blame the situation or the circumstances or someone else for their misfortune. Those people, always find something else that is to blame and rarely is it the person himself.

The same is true in communication. How many times have you tried to explain something to someone and have that person not understand what you are saying? So you explain it again and still they don't understand you. Sometimes we think the other person is being thickheaded! Maybe, just maybe, it could be that we aren't communicating effectively. So instead of telling the other person, "No, you don't understand," maybe we should take responsibility for our own communication and say, "I haven't explained myself clearly."

What I Learned

The outcome of what I do or say or communicate is my responsibility. I accept that. It also helps me feel I'm in greater control over my actions and, more importantly, their outcome.

My Personal Lesson #22: The Desire to Always Want to Get Better

Call it a passion, a drive, or part of my determination, but I have an intense desire to constantly improve myself. That's probably the reason I choose to speak in public, to give seminars and conduct courses, because it keeps me sharp. When you stand up in front of a group of people and give them a message or facilitate a session or teach them something, you better know your stuff. It's tough sometimes, because you will be challenged. There is often someone in the audience or in your class who will challenge you. Those people, even though they can sometimes be disruptive to the rest of the group, are to be thanked, because they only make you better.

New situations that you are not used to, situations that make you feel uncomfortable, venturing outside your comfort zone, makes you better. The more you do it, the more your comfort zone expands. People who achieve great things have often done it by venturing outside their comfort zone.

And venturing outside your comfort zone is related to one's capacity to live in uncertain circumstances. There is a difference between not wanting to fail and having the desire to succeed, or rather in playing not to lose versus playing to win. The latter in both cases is proven to be a much healthier attitude and more conducive to the art of achievement.

What I Learned

Any time I find myself outside my comfort zone that usually means I am learning new things. How I perceive that situation has everything to do with how much I take away from it. Look at it from a positive angle and try to always pull out the best of every situation. Turn the negatives into positives. Turn the downside into something useful.

CHAPTER 3

Your Turn to Write Your Story

I promised myself that I would use these lessons to the best of my ability throughout the rest of my life and to go for what I wanted without holding back. A friend of mine, Roberto Re, who has a training company in Italy and with whom I sometimes collaborate, once said something I never forgot: You already have all the resources inside of yourself that you need to be successful. I believe that. What about you?

Now it's your turn. I invite you to go through the same exercise I just did. You will learn new things about yourself. You will see things that you have forgotten. You might even see some things from a different perspective than you did when they happened. But most importantly, you will discover things that will serve as fuel to project you forward. Just remember that whatever you decide to do in life, the better command you have of yourself, the better you know yourself, the more realistic your perspective will be about where you need to go and how you're going to get there.

If you don't feel comfortable for some reason writing your story, just answer the questions outlined in the "Soul-Searching Exercise" section. My advice, though, is to write the whole story.

By the way, I subscribe to many newsletters, because I like to learn new things. The other day, I received an article called "Defining Moments," by Mark Susnow, a former trial attorney who changed his life around and is now a life coach, speaker, and group facilitator. He wrote about how you can learn from certain moments in your life and how "those moments help you create clarity about your life purpose and your life values." At the end of his article, he wrote the following:

> Bet if you reflect back upon your life, you will discover your own defining moments. After you have revisited them, build upon them to help you discover your destiny. Imagine making a decision today or tomorrow that can potentially define the direction your life takes in the future. What will this decision be? When will you make it? Visit Mark's Web site at www.InspirePossibility.com.

Soul-Searching Exercise

Get yourself an 8 x 10 notepad and find a quiet place where you will not be interrupted and write the story of your life. Break it down like I did in the previous chapter. It is a great way to review your life to date and to notice things you might have missed during the journey. It's important to reflect and ponder life, to look for clues that will help you see if you are doing yourself justice and to help discover what it is you really should be doing. After you have written your story, try to answer the following questions:

1.   What do you think you are here on this earth to accomplish? In other words, what's your purpose in life?

2.   What about you is special?

3.   What do you have to offer this world?

4.   What are the ten greatest successes in your life (as you see them)?

5.   What do you love to do (not just work-related)?

6.   Is there a cause you are passionate about (save the whales, poverty around the world, etc.)?

7.   What aspects of your job do you really enjoy? What don't you enjoy?

8.   What are your hobbies? Could you turn them into a profession? (You probably can.)

9.   Are there certain issues or problems that keep coming up in your life?

10.   What would you like people to say about you after you die?

11.   What are your values? What do you want to stand for?

12.   What legacy would you like to leave behind?

13.   What would you like to accomplish before you die?

14.   If you could do anything in this world and know you would succeed, what would it be?

15.   What was your childhood like?

16.   What was family life like?

17.   What is your relationship like with family members?

18.   When was your first sexual experience? What was it like?

19.   What are your greatest disappointments?

20.   What emotions do you experience most often?

21.   Who are the people you love the most?

22. Who are the people who push you over the limit, annoy you, upset you, make you feel uncomfortable?

23. What is it that makes you happy?

24. What is the happiest period of your life?

25. What is the saddest period of your life?

26. What is your greatest love story? What was it about that person that made him/her special?

27. What five things are you really good at? Why?

28. What are you not very good at? Why not?

29. How would you describe yourself as a person?

30. What motivates you?

31. What can people learn from you?

32. Do you smoke, drink, use drugs? Why? What do they do for you?

33. What things are you afraid of? Why?

34. What are your values?

35. How do you feel about your life in general?

36. Do you consider yourself more of an optimist or a pessimist? Justify your answer.

37. If you want to become an actor or if you already are, what is it that sets you apart from others in your field?

There are many more questions to answer if you really want to dig deep and pull out a serious life direction. If you want to do that, there are many programs in bookstores and on the Internet that will guide you through the process of creating a vision for yourself. Here are two Internet sources that I think are very good, as they are simple and user-friendly:

*www.livesthatmatter.com: A free e-course that guides you step by step through the process of gaining more clarity over what you really want in life.

*www.boundlessliving.com: A good program that deals with the laws of attraction and how to use them in order to get better results in life.

What have you learned about yourself after doing this exercise? If your answer is "nothing," then consider going back and taking more time to go into greater depth. There must be something you can take with you on your journey.

KEY FACTOR # 2

Creating The Necessary Motivation: Making Things Happen!

"There are three kinds of people in this world. There is the kind of person who sits around and waits for something to happen. There is the kind of person who hopes and wishes and prays that something will happen. And then there is the kind of person who makes things happen. Which kind of person are you?"

Dr. Gene Carpenter
Former Head Football Coach
Millersville University of Pennsylvania

CHAPTER 4

Figuring Out What You Really Want In Life And In Your Career

Project yourself into the future. You are eighty-seven years old and sitting on the couch in the living room of your house—the house you'll give to your kids when you pass on. Your grandchildren, and maybe even their children, are sitting around you. The children ask you to tell them a story. They enjoy your stories. They always have. Of course, you are more than happy to oblige them; after all, this is your family! Your offspring! You've told them many stories over the years. This time, however, they want to hear a different story—the story of your life. They all wait eagerly for you to begin.

What will you say, honestly? Consider what you would really like to say and not what you think you should say. For example, instead of something like, "I worked at a job that I didn't like for 40 years; I saved some money but wasn't able to take as many extravagant vacations as I would have liked. I bought a house and just basically lived a modest life as a responsible citizen." Maybe you'd like to say something else. Maybe you'd like to say that, at your current age—thirty, forty, whatever—you changed your life.

Now, wouldn't that make for a much more interesting story?

Here's another question: When you're in your eighties, how will you feel if you continued to live your current life and never followed your dreams? If you never had the nerve to go after that "something" that could have made you happy? Something that could have dramatically improved your quality of life, but you kept doing what you were doing because it was "safe."

Some people believe that we, like cats, have nine lives. That when we die, we will come back and have another shot at "it." Some people believe that once you set your course in life, you must stay that course until the end, no matter how good or bad it is. Some people believe they were meant to do something in life and that there is nothing else in "the script" but that.

If you asked ten people the questions I asked you at the beginning of this chapter, what do you think they would say? Let me tell you. Six out of ten will tell you they are not truly happy. And when you ask them what they would like to do, many will say they do not know, but they can spend fifteen minutes telling you what it is they don't like about their current situation. Sound familiar? Let me tell you something, folks. It doesn't have to be that way! Just as there are many people who are unhappy with different aspects of their lives, there is a small percentage of people who love their occupation; they are happy with many aspects of their lives; when they get up in the morning to go to work, they are excited and energized. When was the last time you felt that way about going to work? When was the last time you felt good about your life situation?

The bottom line is, there are millions of people in this world who are fortunate enough to know what makes them happy and to be doing it every day. You can be one of those people.

A long time ago, someone said, "The best way to predict your future is to create it." Henry Ford said, "Those who believe they can and those who believe they can't are both right."

And, finally, someone else taught us the inevitable truth that says, "If we continue to do the same things we've always done, we can only expect to get the same results." The question is, Are those the results you want to continue getting?

Finding out what you really want from your life, instead of just going through the motions, is such a good feeling and it is easier than you think! It is possible to achieve what you want and to live the life you want. Wouldn't you like to experience that?

Why This Section?

So if this book is for actors then why did I insert this section? Because I recommend you do a soul check and ask yourself why you are doing what you're doing. Why have you chosen to become an artist? Be completely honest with yourself. Otherwise, you could be doing yourself a great disservice and, more importantly, wasting time in your life.

You are probably sure that you want to be an artist, but are you sure you want this to be your professional life's main focus? Could there be something else into which you'd like to integrate your artistic skills? Or are you chasing a dream that really isn't what your heart desires? Are you doing it to spite someone? Doing it for someone else? Because you think this line of work is the only thing you know? Because your friends and family told you this is what you're right for? And so on. Just checking. Bear with me on this and keep on reading.

If you are afraid you might discover something you don't really want to, I know how you feel. When I was fifteen, my first girlfriend's name was Jeanie. I had sex for the first time with this girl. I was in love. I wanted her more than anything, and I just knew she was right for me. Thinking back, I realize she was a little too fast for me, but I wanted her so much! She knew more about sex than I did, and she had already had boyfriends before. I was still wet behind the ears.

My sister-in-law met her and told me she didn't think my relationship with Jeanie would last very long. I was crushed that she would even say something like that. That's not what I wanted to hear! She was older than I was, and she obviously saw something in our relationship or in Jeanie that I didn't see. That bothered me because I didn't want it to be true. I loved that girl, after all. I didn't listen to her and kept investing myself deeper and deeper into the relationship. As I did that, the relationship began to fade. Jeanie cheated on me with her previous boyfriend, and I found out and was crushed again. I went back to my sister-in-law with my tail between my legs. Her eyes just said, "I told you so." I was distraught. I asked her how she knew. She said that she could see it a mile away and wondered how I didn't. She hugged me and told me that one day I would find someone else, and she was right.

Why am I telling you this story? Sometimes it's good to listen to good advice. Our parents often give us good advice when we're growing up, but we don't want to listen because we think we know better. There's the old saying, "The older you get, the smarter your parents get." My advice is to ask yourself the questions, "Why am I doing what I'm doing?", "Why did I decide to become an artist?" "Why have I chosen the career I have?"

If the answer is anything other than your genuine love for the craft or for your profession, let that be a red flag. Maybe you need to rethink whether that's the right thing for you. On the other hand, if you are 110 percent sure, then Godspeed!

Clarifying Your Vision As an Actor

Here are more questions you might want to ask yourself:

1. How long have you been an actor?

2. Have you been working constantly or has it been on and off?

3. Have you been studying to improve? Taking classes regularly? Seeing a coach?

4. Have you been going to good schools or just sporadically taking workshops?

5. Do you have a strategy for how to market yourself as an actor?

6.   Is your marketing strategy working? If so, what is working well for you and what should you continue to do? What isn't working for you, and what should you stop doing? What else could you be doing to market yourself that you haven't tried yet?

7.   Do you have a plan for advancing your career as an actor? If you don't have one, why not? Have you ever had one? If you do, are you following it? How often do you monitor that plan to make sure you stay on track?

8.   Do you have an entrepreneurial spirit?

9.   Do you know what it takes to run a successful business?

10.   Do you usually get things done on time or are you a procrastinator?

11.   Are you aware that being an actor is like running a business and that many successful actors know how to do that?

12.   Are you doing anything innovative to try and get recognition as an actor from the right people?

13.   Have you only been going to forums where you can meet casting directors and agents, rather than studying and taking classes?

So what makes me qualified to ask such questions when I myself am in the first years of my career? Good question. I'm continuing to do research and work the beat. I've been talking to casting directors, agents, managers, actors, teachers, and coaches; reading trade papers; visiting Web sites; going to school and taking classes and workshops; going to forums; and going on auditions. I have a manager and am freelancing with agents. I'm an active subscriber to Web sites that provide casting and other resources for actors. I see what's offered and do submissions and mailings. I call meetings with my agents and manager to discuss what we can do together to get me seen and help me get booked.

I combine all that information with my fifteen-plus years of business management. I'm studying successful working actors, and I know why they are successful, modeling their behavior and their habits and enjoying some modest success.

However, the concepts in the first four sections of this book are the first things you must do, regardless of what career you choose. I know that many successful actors do different things to meet the people they need to meet, that they are prepared, and that they have the same qualities I talk about throughout this book. I have reached many important goals throughout my life, and I know what it takes. Part of it is modeling successful behavior. You need to have the skills necessary to be competitive in your chosen field, but the rest of the formula for achievement is the same no matter what area you are interested in. Will I need a stroke of luck? Maybe, maybe not. But I am already positioning myself for success and am already getting results. I'm getting these results partly because I make things happen. That gives me the confidence to say it will only be a matter of time before I reach where I want to go.

If you answered no to most of the preceding questions, perhaps you do not yet know what you need to do to be successful, in general terms. Could it be that you lack the necessary motivation? Don't worry, though. It is still possible! That's common and it could be a sign that this is not what you really want. Many people play the lottery because they want to be rich, but they don't want to work to become rich. They want the money to just fall into their laps. It could happen, but the chances are very remote. As competitive as the acting world is today, getting lucky—being discovered—is possible but not probable.

"There are three kinds of people in this world. There is the kind of person who sits around and waits for something to happen. There is the kind of person who hopes and wishes and prays that something will happen. And then there is the kind of person who makes things happen. Which kind of person are you?"

Dr. Gene Carpenter
Former Head Football Coach
Millersville University of Pennsylvania

Don't Create an Illusion

If you answered yes to Question 13, then you could be just deluding yourself. I recently participated in an evening forum to which ten agents and casting directors had been invited. There was a question-and-answer session, a chance to audition in front of the panel, and a brief one-on-one session with each of the panelists. During the wait time (there were more than eighty people), there were also seminars and workshops offered. I participated in an on-camera workshop for soap operas.

After I did my scene, I received compliments from the casting director who conducted the workshop as well as from some participants. Some of the participants asked me how I was so relaxed in front of the camera and how I was able to create an environment that wasn't there. I told these individuals that those were things I learned at the school where I study. (I'm very humble, because I know that I have a lot more to learn.) I then asked them where they were taking classes. They said they hadn't started taking classes yet. When I asked them how long they have been acting, their answers ranged from six months to three years. I was baffled! I thought to myself, "How does someone think that they can meet with casting directors and agents without a basis of preparation to act?" Then I realized that there are many actors who do this, hoping to get that break. Those who do are playing the lottery, hoping to win! It is not probable that that will happen. Going up in front of casting directors and agents before you are prepared could ruin your chances to meet these same people again in the near future. I have done it, too, and if I could do it over again, I would spend more time preparing and getting solid technique. Therefore, instead of being in a hurry, take time to prepare, get educated. It takes more time, but it will be well worth it in the end.

> *"If I have three hours to cut down a tree, I would use the first hour to sharpen the ax."*
>
> *Abraham Lincoln*

Sometimes the preparation can seem like a waste of time, and when we see unprepared people getting jobs, we think we can do it too. It's better to take a step backward in order to take two or three steps forward. Get your training, be patient, and if you are diligent and determined and have a method to achieve what you want, then good things will happen.

If you have been puttering along for years, not really achieving anything significant, landing any important jobs, or studying like you should, there's a reason why. You can either continue what you're doing, or you can try and figure out what you must do to get what you really want.

"I Don't Know" Is Not an Acceptable Answer!

It's really important that you don't let yourself get away with answering "I don't know" to any of those questions above. Don't let "I don't know" stop you from living your dreams! If you accept that answer from yourself, you will not find the answers you need.

"I don't know" is laziness. "I don't know" is an excuse not to think anymore. It is not an answer but a dead end. It weakens you. It means surrender. It sucks the life out of you year after year because you have gotten so used to saying it—about everything—and you don't even realize it.

Many people will say, "This is interesting reading," and then never do anything about it. Either that, or they'll say something like, "Makes sense what Anthony wrote. I'll think about it." The fact is, most people never look for the answers. They continue to play the lottery, because it's the easy way to go. Look yourself in the mirror and tell yourself the truth. But don't let yourself get away with "I don't know"! Maybe you don't know the answer to a question in a given moment, but that doesn't mean you won't find it. Get in the habit of saying, "I don't know in this moment, but I will find the answer." Then do just that! And don't stop until you do.

After you write your life story, ponder it thoroughly, and answer the questions, go back and reflect on the answers to the questions regarding your craft. See if things don't make a bit more sense now.

The Conscious vs. The Subconscious

It is important to align our conscious self with our subconscious self. Sometimes we tell ourselves we want to do things, but our subconscious blocks us and keeps us from achieving what our conscious mind is telling us. Here is an example once again from my life. I left the corporate world to pursue my dreams. I kept telling myself that I wanted to leave Italy and return to the States. I had grown tired of living in Italy; I didn't feel comfortable there. I always felt like an outsider and a foreigner. If I went out with acquaintances for dinner or a drink, most often we would talk about Italian politics, which I have no interest in, or we would talk about soccer, which I hate. It was difficult to find anyone who wanted to talk about the NBA or the NFL or who could relate with me about life in New York or in the States; it was difficult finding anyone who had even gone to college in the United States or who was interested in the same things I was or even someone who just spoke my language. So, I began to make preparations for that move. That was what my conscious mind was telling me. My subconscious mind was holding me back, because I still had my son here, who I love very dearly and who I didn't want to leave. This strong subconscious desire not to leave my son was sabotaging my efforts to strive for what I thought I really wanted.

I found that I was slow to move forward with my plan, and I was only half-committed to my actions. Consequently, there were half-finished projects and profound frustration. I began to hate Italy. This was when I first contemplated moving back to the United States. I had always thought of the situation as either black or white. I thought I must either stay in Italy or move back to the States. The reason for the either/or in my mind was of course because I did not want to abandon my son.

And then I woke up and started asking myself questions that helped me focus on a solution to my dilemma rather than on the problem itself. I asked myself if it was possible to have some of both worlds. I adopted a strategy that gave me the flexibility to go back and forth between both countries during a period of a few years. I would first set up my consulting business and a small

Internet marketing business, which would allow me the flexibility and the earning power to go back to New York and Los Angeles, study acting periodically, and write. Once I did that, I began to achieve what I wanted and move forward with greater clarity and conviction; thus, I got swifter results. I felt better about my choices and am now at peace in my soul.

Is your subconscious sabotaging your efforts and keeping you from getting what you want? Are you trying and trying to achieve something but things always come up to hinder your efforts? Think about it and ask yourself if you are in alignment. Then ask yourself once again, "Is this what I really want to do?" If the answer is yes, I do want to be an artist (or whatever you have chosen), then ask yourself another question: "Why am I answering no to questions 2 through 12 in the section above, 'Clarifying Your Vision As an Actor'? Be honest! If you don't soon start answering yes to those questions, your path to reach your goal, whatever it is, will be much more difficult and will probably take you longer—if you get to achieve the success you desire at all.

You might not like your own answers to those questions. You might be convinced that you want to act or dance or whatever, but your heart and your soul might be saying something different. If they are saying two different things, don't ignore them. They just might be right. It's a sign that you need to dig deeper and find out why. You will save much time, money, effort, and, most importantly, you will be at greater peace with yourself.

Something else to consider is whether your passion is all you want to do. In my case, after much thought, I discovered that acting is an integral part of my speaking and television-hosting career. If I get that big break as an actor, I will certainly take it, but my main goal is television hosting and speaking at events around the subject of my books.

Clarify Your Ideas Even Further

Since starting this book, hopefully by now you have an idea of what you really want to do in life or feel that you are on the right track. This answer could come to you very easily, but usually it requires much thought. It may take days, weeks, or months. Keep asking yourself the question until you find the answers you want. Why do I talk so much about what you want out of life instead of focusing more on your career and professional life? Because the clearer the "bigger picture" is for you, the more clarity you can have in whatever field you choose. That's a fact.

Remember that your goal must be specific! It is difficult to plan where you are going if you don't have a clear destination. A captain of a ship always knows where he is going before he sets sail. As a personal example I've mentioned previously, I quit my corporate job some years ago to pursue my dreams. The first step in my plan was to set up a business that would give me the flexibility to set my own schedule and to make as much money as possible in one day's work. At that particular point in time, I decided consultancy and training seminars were the best way to get what I wanted by utilizing some of the know-how and resources that I had at my disposal. I could not quit a good job to simply "be a consultant." I had to ask myself this series of questions:

1. Do I really understand what it means to be a consultant?
2. What skills does a good consultant need to have? What are the characteristics of a good consultant?
3. What does the market look like in which I will operate? How big is it? Who are the key players? Who is my competition?
4. What kind of financial resources do I have to begin this business?
5. What industry standards do I need to know?
6. What kind of consultant do I want to be?
7. Do I need a skill set that I don't currently have?
8. Do I only want to consult, or do I want to do courses and seminars as well?
9. What kinds of topics will I cover in my work (i.e., leadership, strategic planning, sales marketing, etc.)?
10. Who will my customers be?
11. Where will I work? In Italy? The United States? In which region of the country? What industries will I work for?
12. How much will I charge?
13. How much money would I like to make? Daily? Monthly?
14. How many days per month would I like to work?
15. What kind of quality of life would I like to have?
16. What will my sales process look like?
17. Will I work alone or will I have employees?
18. If I have employees, how many, what will they do, and how much will I pay them? Where will I look for them?
19. How much will I invest in my new business? In what areas will I invest?
20. Where and how will I find my customers?

21. Will I work only for my company or will I also freelance for other companies who do the same thing?

22. What kinds of technical tools will I need to do my job (i.e., projector, computer, etc.)?

23. Do I need a Web site? What will it need to provide? What kind of information? What function will it serve?

24. What will the company name be?

25. How can I involve my son in the business?

26. How will I travel to my accounts?

27. Do I need an office?

These are just some of the questions I asked myself. The more specific you are in asking yourself what you want, the easier it will be to get it.

I'm sure you've heard of SMART goals—Specific, Measurable, Achievable, Relevant, Timely. The more specific and detailed you are about what you want, the better your chances are of reaching your goal. If you don't know exactly where you are going, how do you expect to get there?

CHAPTER 5

Overcoming Your Resistance to Change

You have two choices: you can either continue to not have the time or the money to invest in your craft, to get off work for auditions, classes, preparation, or practice, or you can do something differently. Perhaps you've heard that the definition of *insanity* is to do what you have always done and expect different results. If you continue doing what you're doing, you only need to ask yourself, "Where will I be five years from now? Will I be any closer than I am now to getting what I want out of my career? Or are you doing what many artists do and play the career lottery and wait to get lucky, thinking that having sent in headshots and résumés to casting directors and agents is enough? Do you just talk to people who have connections and put all your eggs in that basket, hoping they will do something for you?

I'm being provocative because I want you to think. Whatever you are doing for your career, ask yourself, "What more can I do?" "Is it enough?" And if the answer to the latter question is no, then ask yourself, "What am I going to do about it?"

Whether you choose to go through the actions I suggest in this book or go through another type of course, take some seminar, follow some program, or get a coach, you must open your heart and your spirit to receive and to learn and most importantly to change. If you don't, your chances for success will not be in line with the full potential you have within you.

I have conducted numerous seminars and courses over the years and given many presentations. By the same token, I have participated in many. There are folks who, especially in companies where someone else has decided that they must attend the seminar, come with their arms folded and legs crossed and head back as if to say, "Okay, let's hear what you have to say. I've tried other programs and they never work for me. I'm here hoping that this one will be different." Deep down, though, they really don't believe it will work. In the courses I conduct, I address this issue immediately. If you come to a seminar or training session with that attitude, chances are it won't work. And you know what else I tell them? I don't want them in my classroom with that attitude!

Get the Most out of Everything You Do!

I also see people who come passively to seminars. They sit there and don't take notes, don't pay attention. What a waste! If you invest the time and the money to go through a program, then why not open yourself up, at least for the time you are there, to the possibility that what you're being taught just might work? Open yourself up to learn as much as you can while you're there. It's worth a try, isn't it? Let yourself go. Play. Be open. Participate fully. Interact. Ask questions. Be inquisitive. Ponder your options. Apply the information to your own situation. Try and walk your situation through the process to see what comes out of it.

If you do those things even with this book, you will make progress. If you close yourself to all the possibilities out there, you will find yourself back at square one with all the other strugglers. It's your choice.

Have the courage to step out of your comfort zone, that sphere of comfort you have created over the years in which you feel safe and without worry or stress. If you really want to make a change in your life, a big change, an important change, you must adopt a different way of thinking and acting. One of the best ways to do this is doing things that help you step out of your comfort zone. Good things can come from acting within your comfort zone. Great things come from acting outside of it.

Your Comfort Zone

What is the comfort zone? It is different for all of us. For one person it could be staying at home and reading or watching television instead of going out to clubs. It could mean going to the same café with the same group of friends on Sunday mornings for brunch. It could mean going to the gym or for a run or engaging in your favorite sport with your buddies. It could mean doing something alone or always being around people. It depends on you. Everyone's comfort zone is different.

When a very reserved or timid person comes into contact with a group of people, they might feel out of their comfort zone or feel that their comfort zone is stretched. That person's natural instinct might then be to get back home as soon as possible, back into their comfort zone. It could be pure torture for that same person to appear in front of a group of people and give a speech. For someone else, this situation might be right in the middle of their comfort zone. Your comfort zone consists of the things that normally you do that make you feel comfortable, the things you usually do that help you to feel "in your element", What about you? What are the things that are within your comfort zone?

Some teachers will make you do what they call "a moment of public solitude" or "private moments." In these moments, an actor must be able to completely block out the rest of the group while doing something in front of the class that they would normally do in the privacy of their own home (no sex, masturbating, or going to the bathroom was allowed).

These exercises are designed to remove one from their comfort zone while at the same time stretching the zone to such an extent that these things become normal. Let's face it. If a person can't be natural in front of his peers, in a scene he can choose, then acting, singing, or performing in general will probably be a difficult undertaking. If we're not comfortable in front of the group, on stage, or in front of the camera, it will show. The only way to work through this is to continue doing it until it becomes comfortable and natural.

This same concept can be applied to goals and the actions needed to accomplish those goals, actions a person might not be used to doing.

You're Only Cheating Yourself

There were times during football practice in college when we had to run an exercise called "stations." There were seven stations spread out in the different ends of the field, where we had to do different drills such as driving a heavy sled, high-stepping through ropes that were set up in a certain pattern, performing concentration drills, and so forth. All the drills lasted two minutes and were situated around the field approximately twenty-five yards apart. The head coach, Dr. Gene Carpenter, stood in the middle of the field and blew the whistle after each two-minute period, which was a sign for us to move to the next station. We were expected to give 100 percent at each station and then sprint to the next station when the whistle blew.

You can imagine how we felt after finishing all the stations. It was an endurance exercise, but it was also an exercise in discipline—physical as well as mental. We knew the coach couldn't watch every player at the same time and that the other coaches couldn't keep constant watch on all of us, either. So what did some players do, including me sometimes, when the coach wasn't looking? We loafed. We slowed down even just for a second or two to catch our wind, because it was tough, because it was too much, because we needed a break, because we were tired. Knowing this, he would yell out, "Men, if you're not giving this exercise 110 percent, you're cheating your teammates, because they might need your endurance in the fourth quarter of the game. But most of all, men, you're cheating yourselves!"

Sometimes we know what we should be doing, what we need to do in order to get what we want or to achieve a goal, but for some reason we don't do it or we tell ourselves that today I'll rest and do it tomorrow. Instead of getting up at eight to do our drop-offs or write those postcards and letters, we get up at ten because we stayed out late partying the night before. So what happens? The cards and letters get pushed back to the next day. Or we fail to budget adequately and spend our money foolishly; leaving us without the money to take that much-needed class, and we end up having to wait until the next time it will be offered. There are many parallels to this example in our everyday lives. I realize that not everyone is like that, but as they say, if the shoe fits… Discipline is an important characteristic of those who achieve great results.

You know whether or not you're doing what you should to reach your goals. If you are not, then there is no one to blame but you. There was a saying back when I was at Nike among the many employees who were runners: "Either you ran today or you didn't." There are no excuses. At times you would hear someone say that they didn't have time to run or train that day. A friend of mine once said, "Saying you don't have time is another way of saying that it is not that important to you, because if it were important enough, you would find the time." No matter what time you go to bed or how much sleep you get, for example, you would have gotten up earlier and gone for a run, because it was important. People find the time to do the things that are really important to them. Coach Carpenter used to tell us, "Excuses are like assholes. Everyone has one and they all stink!"

CHAPTER 6

Going Forward

There was once a man who was walking through the forest one day. He was lost and the farther he walked into the forest, the more lost he became. He came upon a fork in the path, where he found an old man. He asked the old man, "Excuse me, sir. I'm lost. Could you please tell me which way I should go?" The old man asked, "Where are you going, young man?" The man replied, "I just need to get out of here. I'm lost. Can you please just tell me which way I should go?" The old man replied, "If you can't tell me where you are going, then either path will do."

There are a few things you must do to make sure that you have a better chance of getting to where you want to go. We often find ourselves in a situation where we either accept the change that someone else imposes upon us or where we effect the change we want. We sometimes stammer and hesitate and procrastinate when having to make decisions. As I said before, not making a decision is a decision in itself. Before you go forward, especially if you want to move quickly and get results as fast as possible, then you need to be clear about where you are going.

Change the Way You Think

If you want different results, you *must* think in a different way than the way you are thinking now. In a six-week intensive acting course I took last summer at the Ward Studio in New York, our movement teacher and actor Grant Neale asked us a question that I never forgot and that I use daily to motivate myself to get better results than the ones I'm already getting: "How many different ways are there to get someone to do what you want them to do?" We did exercises around that idea that really made us think.

We discussed and did exercises around just four of the many ways there are to influence someone: entice, plead, demand and encourage. At times we have our standard way of doing things and we think, "That's the way I've always done it." Anything that isn't in line with the way we have always done things takes us out of our comfort zone and doesn't feel right. But that's what you must do to start getting different results! In the beginning it doesn't feel right, but in the end you expand your comfort zone so that things that seemed strange in the past now seem normal.

Getting to the Point of Feeling Comfortable

They say that it takes about twenty-eight days to form new habits if you work on it every day. Try this:

Have you ever tried putting your watch on your other wrist? Try it. How does it feel? A little strange, huh? That's how it feels when we start applying new methods and new techniques to getting what we want. Once we do it repeatedly, it becomes natural and less strange. If you put your watch on that wrist every day for a month, don't you think that it will start to feel normal? Or how about auditions? Do you remember the first auditions you ever did? How did you feel? A little nervous? Did that nervousness affect your performance? When you are in a groove and audition regularly, the nervousness usually subsides, because you are used to it. You feel more prepared and that feels good. You've expanded your comfort zone.

For me it is the same in my consulting and speaking business, which I do because I like it and because it helps keep me sharp for performing. In the beginning, before I had a lot of experience, I was just an okay speaker, but now, after having given hundreds of presentations and conducted many courses and seminars, I am completely different from when I was as a novice.

I'm always trying new things and have already built the structure around one of my future books, which is aimed at the many different ways there are to present concepts and to communicate messages. The last thing I want that book to be is just another public-speaking text. There are an infinite number of ways to present, and some of them you will see me do on the Internet. It is a mentality that helps you create different ways of getting what you want or of resolving an issue, always wanting to improve and to come up with something new that will set you apart from all the rest.

So, if you are not getting the results you want in your career and you are continuing to do what you are doing, it is improbable that you will soon start getting better results unless you just plain get lucky. You must change your approach. To do this you must first change your way of thinking and get used to thinking that way until it becomes part of your comfort zone. .If you do, you will be able to move much more quickly towards achieving your results.

Think as the Person You Want to Become

"No problem can be resolved at the same level of thought at which it was created."

Einstein

You are going to create a plan around your vision of the future, around something that you want to achieve. The point here is that you will be hard-pressed to do it thinking as you always have. If your goal, for example, is to become rich, then you will certainly not get there by thinking like a poor person. You need to think like rich people think. If you don't know how they think and if that is really your goal, then you need to find out!

Now let's narrow it down to something with regard to your career as an actor. Do any of the following sentences reflect your situation?

- You are not being sent out on many auditions.

- When you do get sent out, you rarely get called back.

- You don't have an agent and are having trouble finding one.

- You are able to book jobs, but there have been instances in which you weren't able to keep them.

- You don't have many industry contacts.

- You can't seem to meet that industry professional you would really like to meet.

- You're sending out your materials—audition tapes, head shots, and résumés—but you're not getting any response or you're not getting the types of responses you would like.

- You don't have the money to take classes as often as you would like, so you just take a workshop every now and again instead of going to a school like you know you need to. It's been your situation for months. Years.

- You are having difficulty getting off work for auditions, because your boss doesn't support you.

- Whenever you do have auditions, you find it difficult to prepare because of the time you must spend at work, or you're too tired, or you can't seem to hook up with a partner who can help you.

- Oftentimes you have to work at a club or restaurant until the wee hours of the morning and go into your audition looking like a zombie.
- You don't have the cash to make a show-reel or audition tape.

These are just examples. Your case might be similar or completely different. You might even be too new at this to have done any of these things. It really doesn't matter. The question is, if you have issues to resolve, obstacles to overcome that are impeding your progress, what are you going to do about them? Remember, as you go through this process, "I don't know" isn't a valid answer! Most people need a wake-up call before they begin to take action. Do you? When they finally take stock of their situation and stop thinking that these things are normal and that everything is based on the luck of the draw, they might intensify their efforts, because there is greater probability in numbers. The more I do of the same thing, the greater chance I have of getting results. On the other hand, there are people who continue at exactly the same rate— for example, sending out the same number of mailings in exactly the same way hoping they will get different and better results. More often than not, these are not the answers to their difficulties and challenges.

Anthony Robbins says that, "Achieving goals by themselves will never make us happy in the long term; it's who you become, as you overcome the obstacles necessary to achieve your goals, that can give you the deepest and most long-lasting sense of fulfillment." So the question I ask you now is, "What kind of person will you have to become to get what you want, to have the kind of career you want?" You must begin to think like the person who already has achieved the things you want. In this way, you can increase your probability of success.

Effort and Results

Think about the finals of the 100-meter track-and-field events in the Olympics over the years. Have you ever seen a photo finish? Of course you have. At times the races are so close that the first three are within hundredths of a second of each other. It's really a shame, because there can be only one winner. One could safely say that all three are great athletes and deserve to win. But there is only one gold medal. Unfortunately, people don't usually remember second and third place. They only remember who wins. In situations like the photo finishes, oftentimes winning can come down to something very simple but that proves to be the determining factor. It could be something as simple as leaning at the finish or sticking their neck out farther than the person who finishes second. And that tiny action made all the difference in the world.

It turned a great result of being second in the world into an extraordinary result of being number one.

Level of Effort put forth	=	Results Achieved
Putting forth 360°, extraordinary effort. Think about the sign on the wall in the gym in the movie 'Million Dollar Baby'. Do you remember what it said? If not, ask someone who saw it.	Will get you	Extraordinary Results
Putting forth above average effort	Will get you	Good results
Putting forth an average effort in which you do only what is necessary	Will get you	Mediocre results
Putting forth a mediocre effort	Will get you	Poor results

Find a Mentor

You know, it's not always necessary to go it alone. There are other people who have gone before you, many of whom would be glad to help you. All you have to do is ask. This doesn't mean getting them to do your legwork for you. That is not a good idea. Doing that will neither help you grow nor please the person you ask. For example, it can quickly turn people off if you ask them to introduce you to their contacts or casting directors or agents, especially if they have never seen your work.

When I say ask for help, what I really mean is find a mentor. You must be able to walk on your own two feet. A mentor can steer you in the right direction, help you learn from their experience, explain certain things that might keep you from making the same mistakes they did, and so on. It certainly depends on who you ask.

Remember this: Your goals and what you are trying to accomplish are never going to be as important to anyone else as they are to you. If you are on people too much, always asking for favors, introductions, advice, they might turn away from you or gradually become less available.

You need good communication skills. Are you a good, effective communicator? Use your contacts wisely and sparingly and always have a clear idea of what you want to ask and what type of answer you are looking for so as to take up as little of their time as possible.

We are all human. Sometimes when I don't get the type of answer I want from someone, it is usually because of the way I communicated my request. Figure out what it is you need and shoot for that information.

Get in the habit of seeking out guidance for and not the solutions to your problems. In doing this, you will grow into someone who figures things out for himself.

Ask good questions. (We will go into greater depth on that later on.) Good questions are magical! They are so important. For instance, you might need information on how to effectively promote yourself as an artist. In addition to asking someone how they promote themselves, for example, you could ask how many different ways there are to promote oneself. That question forces them to think about not only the things they do, but also some things they have heard others do and that maybe you could do too. It becomes a sort of mini brainstorming session instead of a person giving you straight-up advice. In that way, maybe without him or her even realizing it, you have also helped them think of something new, you have stimulated them and the next time you come back for more advice, you could just be more welcome than before.

Change the Way You Think

Connect these nine dots with four straight lines without lifting your writing instrument from the paper. (You cannot retrace a line you have already drawn. If you do, you will not be able to complete the task in just four straight lines.) When you are finished connecting all nine dots, they should be interconnected with four straight lines.

• • •

• • •

• • •

How did you do? Still having trouble? Here's a clue: You might be looking for the answer where there is no answer. If you are thinking about how to resolve this problem by staying within the square formed by the nine dots, you will be looking for a long time. You must think outside the box in order to solve this task. (Answer key in the appendix at the end of the book.)

Beliefs and Results

Anthony Robbins teaches us a lot about the characteristics that successful people have in common. There is a "cycle of success" that deals with how important beliefs are and how much they can influence the outcome of any endeavor. It goes like this:

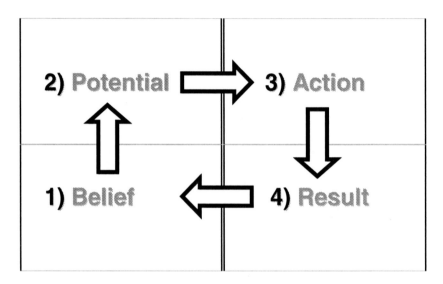

This diagram says that everything we do begins with our point of view with regard to the task we are about to tackle. Our belief in whether or not we think it is possible is crucial in helping to determine the outcome. If you have a task to complete and believe you can accomplish it, you will move on to step two. Step two means that based on the degree to which you believe in your ability to successfully accomplish the task; you will bring into the game a certain amount of your own potential to get the job done. If your belief is low, then the amount of potential you bring will be low; the resources that you awaken inside to help yourself will be few. If instead you have a strong belief, then you will dig deep to bring out as much potential as you have to get the job done.

Then you move on to the actions. The actions you put together to accomplish your goal will be in direct proportion to the strength of your belief and to the amount of your own potential you have brought into the game. If the first two are high, then you will inevitably put together a great strategy to accomplish your goal; otherwise you will not. And finally, these three things are among the determining factors that influence the outcome or the result. If you've worked well, your result will be rewarding. If not, then it will not be.

This happens in life all the time. Some years ago, when I was the sales director for the Italian market for Nike and was in a meeting at a sales conference, our European general manager walked into the room. He told us that we had to begin selling soccer shoes to our customers in the wintertime. The vast majority of the sales force in Europe thought the idea was absolutely ridiculous. They felt that anyone with any knowledge of the soccer market would not even suggest something like that. It had never been done by anyone, not even Adidas, who had been making soccer shoes for many years before Nike came along.

One of my direct reports was my soccer sales manager, who came to me a few days later and said he didn't think it would be possible to get any significant soccer shoes sales in the wintertime. When I hear negativity, I start to boil inside. I knew that it wouldn't be easy, but the only option available was to succeed! I told him to go back to his office and to come see me again in an hour, with a plan, a functional and feasible plan that would have us selling the targeted number of soccer shoes. I told him I didn't want to see him without the plan.

My senior management colleagues and I had our hands full at times with trying to overcome the hindering beliefs surrounding the sale of soccer shoes in the wintertime. With time, however, by first creating high-quality soccer shoes, pushing the sales force, supporting the sales campaign with marketing and getting results, everyone started to believe it was possible, and today it is normal.

The same thing happened back in 1990 when I first started in the company back in Germany. The message that some of my European colleagues wanted to give to our American colleagues in Nike was that "We Europeans don't wear athletic shoes as much as the Americans, so don't expect that Nike will achieve great results selling its shoes in Europe." That was then. Now more than a decade later more than five times as many shoes are sold on the old continent. If we had let that negativity prevail, it could have negatively affected the company's growth or, more probably, some people's jobs would have been at risk!

My quitting my corporate job to pursue my dreams of being an actor and speaker/TV host serves once again as a perfect example. If I had listened to all the negative people who told me not to do it and to stay "in my comfort zone" and that it wasn't possible to do something like that at my age, I would never be where I am today. Worse yet, I might have quit my job anyway and let them influence my belief system, convincing me I wouldn't be able to do it. As a result, the potential and the resources that I would have pulled out of myself would have been few. The strategy, the plan, and the action items that I would have put together to go in the right direction would have been insufficient, and as a result, the outcome would not have been good. In that case, I probably would have said what many people say who go through that process not convinced of what they are doing: "I don't even know why I tried. They were right. I knew it wouldn't be possible anyway!"

Think about Winning

Tony Robbins tells a story in one of his books about how he found himself on the brink of bankruptcy, when an ugly surprise reared its head to the tune of a large, six-figure debt. His team was making preparations to file for bankruptcy, something he refused to accept. While other members of his team were asking how this could have happened and how they were going to get out of that mess, Tony was asking himself how he could not only solve this situation, but also take it a step further and end up better off that he was before. After some serious thought, he decided that to come up with that money by continuing to do what he was doing and by working in the same way that he had always been working was not going to do it. He had to think of a better way. If only he could do more courses and seminars. Wasn't possible because everyone wanted *him* and he was only one man. That's when he came up with the idea of making audio and video course and selling those. That was the key, along with some other strategies he implemented that allowed him to save his company and continue even stronger than before. (By the way, if you haven't read his book "Awaken The Giant Within", you might want to check it out. It's well worth it.)

Could it also be that you do all these things and your result is still not satisfactory? Of course. But that's the time to learn from what happened and analyze it so that you can do better next time. The important thing is to never give up. If your goal is important enough to you, you will persist until you succeed.

If at First You Don't Succeed, Try, Try Again

Remember this. Picasso painted more than 20,000 paintings in his life and only a small percentage of them were ever made public and fewer still became famous. Thomas Edison made over 1,200 attempts before he was successful. Mozart wrote over 2,300 compositions to come up with those that made him famous. And an example from the sports world that speaks to me the most: I saw a poster that had Michael Jordan's face and a quote from him:

> "I've missed more than 9,000 shots in my career. I've lost almost 300 games, 26 times I've been trusted to take the game winning shot and missed. I failed, over and over and over again in my life. And that is why I succeed."

What a great quote!

People don't become good, much less great, at something by simply trying it once or twice. It takes time. What makes someone think that he can become great putting forth less effort than the people I mentioned here? What makes us artists think, for example, that we can just appear in front of a casting director or an agent without having any formal training, without having gone to classes? If we want to be good, it takes work. Hard work. And with hard work comes a payday. If you are lucky, the payday will come even without the hard work. Sure. Anything is possible. But, becoming great without hard work is simply not probable.

Your Universe Will Help You

When you strongly believe that you can do something, everything else falls in place. What Julia Cameron says in her book *The Artist's Way* is worth mentioning again: When you are motivated to go after what you want, the universe will conspire to help you. I have found that to be true. Magical things begin to happen. You might see something while walking down the street that might give you an idea of how to overcome an obstacle or find a solution to help you get closer to your goal. You could hear something on the radio, see a billboard, something in the newspaper, overhear a conversation, have a dream, have a conversation with someone. When you are *really* focused on getting a result, things around you will begin to happen that will help you be successful.

You give it your all putting into operational mode every resource you have and those that others might have to help you. You do things. You might not necessarily have many actions in place to accomplish the task or reach your goal, but you have the ones you need to be successful. You will inevitably get a result of some sort, but the quality of that result obviously depends on how you've worked and how you've planned. If it doesn't meet your expectations, then you must analyze it to see what you can learn for the next time.

The problem at times is that we are often conditioned by the result to such an extent, that if the result is negative, we either throw in the towel or let it affect how we go forward. If you are motivated to reach your goal, you can't let that happen. All the things we are discussing here are to help improve the probability of success. It is not realistic to think that we can be 100 percent successful 100 percent of the time in everything we do, but we can strive for that without being too focused on perfection, which can be a serious setback in terms of time.

"Those who believe they can and those who believe they can't are both right

Henry Ford

Here are four steps to help you strive for greatness on a continuous basis:

1. Open your mind's eye. This can be a life-changing experience. Simply noticing things around you that you have always taken for granted or maybe even never thought of. Sometimes we focus on a certain resource or application of that resource when trying to achieve a goal, and we miss out on other things that are happening around us that could also be important. Some of those things might be unrelated to what you are trying to accomplish, but they could also stimulate you to find a solution that will take you where you want to go. There are things happening to you and affecting you right at this moment that you are probably not thinking about.

For example, do you have any idea what your pulse is at the moment? Think about every part of your body. Has tension accumulated in any one area of your body? Your shoulders maybe? Your back? Your jaw? Are you frowning unnecessarily? How does your back feel leaned against the chair you are sitting on? How do your feet feel in the position they are currently? Are there any other sounds in or outside your room? What are they? Take in everything!

Last year there was a story circulating around the Internet. I even heard it at a seminar and would like to share it with you:

A woman, who happened to be very religious, was at home alone one day when it started to rain heavily. It rained so much that the drains on the street were blocked and the water began to rise. The forecast called for it to continue raining all through the next day. The woman said a prayer and asked God to watch over her and keep her safe. In the meantime, the water continued to rise and the mayor called for the police to go around and evacuate all the homes in the town. A policeman came up to the woman's house in a motorboat and saw that she was at home. He knocked on the window downstairs as the water began to enter the house, seeping under the door. He told her to leave her home and come with him and that he would take her to safety. The woman thanked the man kindly but said that she would stay, because God would keep her safe.

Some hours passed and the water continued to rise. It was so high that the entire ground floor of her house was flooded. She had no choice but to go upstairs. Once again the police department in a bigger boat visited her with other people who had been evacuated from their homes. Again they pleaded with the woman to come with them so that they could take her to safety. Once again she thanked them and told them that God would keep her safe and that she would stay in her home. The men shook their heads as they continued to go and evacuate others. The woman got down on her knees and said another prayer and asked God to keep her safe.

Still more time passed. By this time, the water had risen so high that even the upstairs was flooded and woman was on her roof. For the third time, policemen in a boat pleaded with her to come with them. She said no! She wanted to stay. She insisted that it would stop raining and that God would keep her safe. She once again got down on her knees and prayed for God to keep her safe. A few hours later, the water had gotten so high that it covered the entire house and the woman could not hold on any longer. She drowned.

As she was a devout Christian, she went to Heaven. When she arrived, she met up with God, who welcomed her. But she was curious and had to ask, "Why didn't you save me from the flood? I prayed to you and asked you for help. Why did you let me die out there?!" God replied, "I sent you the police three times to take you away in boats, and you were so stubborn that you just had to stay! Why didn't you listen to those warnings from me?"

The moral of the story: Take in everything, because everything that happens is good for something, which leads me to the next thing: people.

2. Everyone you meet gives you something that will help you achieve your goal. Everyone! It is a gift. Take the time to figure out what it is. Is it something they said? Something they did? Something they did for you or for themselves that stimulates you to think? Sometimes it is obvious. Other times it is not. Take the time to think about what it could be. That in itself is well worth your while.

I took an acting course a couple months ago, and we did an exercise that I will never forget, because it really helped change the way I think. It has helped me develop my creativity, open my mind, and, most importantly, helped me raise the bar on the results that I am getting in my everyday life.

We were paired up in this exercise. The task given to us by our teacher was to tell our partner about a problem that we have in some aspect of our lives, that we have been carrying on our shoulders for some time and that we would like to resolve as quickly and as painlessly as possible. We did that. "And now" he said, "I would like you to give some advice to your partner as to how they might go about resolving that problem." The fact that we might have no experience in the field in which our partner had the problem was not important. We were simply to give insight as to the resolution of our partner's problem from our point of view. Simply give the other person advice. We did that. And then he asked two questions. The first was, "Who feels that they received a valid response from their partner. In other words, who feels like the answer they received was of value." He asked for a show of hands. My partner raised her hand. I did not. I didn't feel like the answer she gave me would help me in any way. Then the teacher asked the question that really made me think. That magical question: "And who received an answer that was a good answer, but who just doesn't know it?" I looked around the room and saw some people, who looked a little puzzled by the question. I smiled inwardly and outwardly, because I knew he was right. He then followed by telling us, "If you want to achieve great things in your life, if you want to be successful, if you want to simply achieve your goals, live the kind of life you want, that is far from the kind of life you are living now, then you must begin to see things differently.

Everyone," he said, "gives you something, their own personal gift to you. If you learn to see things in that way, you will be amazed at the new opportunities you will begin to see, the new paths that will open up to you." From that moment on, I knew I would look at things differently.

Adopting this mentality will help tremendously in the development of your creative mind.

3. Ask yourself, "What needs to happen in order for me to get what I want?" Be very specific in your answer. This is not about what you *think* is possible. It is an exercise in objectivity and in telling yourself what really has to happen in order for you to be successful, no matter who you are or what your level of skill. Anyone who has this goal or wants to achieve this objective must do these things to get it done. This list is what I call your "Key Factors for Success." These are the things that absolutely must happen for you to reach your goal.

One mistake people make in this phase is they begin thinking about their current skill level, their current situation, or their capacity as individuals right now to do a certain task. This limits you and the results you can achieve right from the outset. Instead, think as big as necessary about what needs to happen in order to ensure you reach your goals. Then think about the person you must become in order to achieve those goals. While you are considering these things, don't try to figure out how you will be able to achieve your goals. Simply tell yourself objectively the things that need to happen if you're going to be successful.

4. Now here is the biggest question so far: "What are you willing to do to reach your goal?"

You must identify what sacrifices, if any, you are willing to make now before you begin the journey. This can save you time and money down the road. It's better to know now before you spend a lot of time and energy on your project only to discover later on that you don't want to go any further.

I wrote earlier about my feeling trapped in Italy. As much as I wanted to return to the States, I just couldn't; I couldn't abandon my son, and I didn't even want to consider dragging him away from his mother. Even though she and I have a better relationship now than we did when were married and that she is a great mother, we both know that our son needs both of us. I used to think that the situation was either black or white: Either I stay in Italy or I return to the States. Then, thinking outside the box, I decided on a third alternative: I would try to do both. Spending some time each year in Italy as well as in the States until my son gets a little bigger and can travel to see me.

I had to ask myself, What am I willing to do for what I want? The biggest challenge is being away from him. I talk to him and try my best to help him understand why I go to New York and Los Angeles a couple times a year for some months. When I'm gone, I always communicate with him every day. I have thought of innovative ways to keep in touch with him when I'm away. It's a sacrifice for me and for him.

I'm giving you this example to help you understand that when you decide what it is you really want, you can't really say that you will go for it until you face your biggest challenge or obstacle and overcome it. Deal with it. Then you can say you're ready. Things can come up unexpectedly, but it's important to know what you are willing to do and how far you are willing to go to get what you want.

What are you willing to do to reach your goals as an artist?

Dream Great Dreams

To do the previous exercise successfully, you must know what success looks like. You must visualize it in the smallest detail. This technique can save you. Close your eyes and visualize what things will be like when you have reached your goal. What will have changed? How will it have changed?

The night before our games, Coach Carpenter would tell us to "dream great dreams." He told us that if we could envision ourselves making that great play in the game the next day that we could probably do it. In other words, if you can't see what it is you want, how will you be able to get it?

Let me give you an example. My goal of becoming an actor and speaker/TV host began three years prior to making the big move to leave the corporate world. I knew that at forty-two years old I didn't want to just dive in blindly and rely solely on acting. Realistically I knew that it would not be the easiest thing I have ever done in my life and that I was going to have to make money somehow. I thought that if I wanted to work from nine to five for some company, I could have just stayed with my company and asked for a transfer to LA.

I knew I didn't want to work in bars or clubs or look for temporary work, so first I asked myself what kind of work I wanted to do to make ends meet, work that would enable me to concentrate as much as possible on my craft. I immediately asked myself other questions that helped me decide. I knew that presenting and teaching were two things I really enjoyed. I also considered what resources I already had that would permit me to be a speaker, give presentations, and teach. My background as a sales manager and internal trainer, and my prior speaking experience were the resources I already had that were sharp and ready to be used to make money as soon as I organized myself.

Then I went a step further. I didn't just want to make money; I wanted to create the flexibility I needed so that (1) I could take time off and go to the States a couple times a year to study, (2) I'd be free to go to auditions whenever they pop up, and (3) I could make as much money as possible in the least amount of time and with the least amount of effort. I didn't have the financial resources to invest in real estate, and I hadn't been wise in some of my earlier investments, so I pretty much had to start from scratch, relying on my savings to get started. The result? I ended up founding a corporate training and consulting business, which allowed me to teach, speak at conventions, and plan my business around my schedule.

I visualized what life would be like when I had achieved that goal of setting up and working that business. I envisioned how it would be scheduling my appointments with customers, how I would find them, how long it would take from the first meeting to actually close the sale. I knew who my customers would be and answered all the questions I listed above and more. I actually closed my eyes and saw as clearly as possible what a typical month would look like, my movements, my clients, the meetings, and the seminars and courses. I knew how much I would have to spend for materials, gas, and other business-related costs. I knew how much I would charge customers and for what, and I knew how I would justify those extra charges should a customer challenge me. I have achieved that goal. Now I am working on the next phase of my project, and yes, I am thinking big. Very, very big!

CHAPTER 7

Anything Is Possible

To do a visualization exercise effectively, you must step out of your comfort zone. Think outside the box. Think big, and while writing down all the different ways to achieve your goal, follow the rule that everything is possible. *Everything!*

If you have trouble in the beginning, pull out a piece of paper and write down all the different ways of getting what you want. Really push yourself to answer the question, "How many different ways are there to get what I want?" Give yourself a target of how many of these things you would like to come up with and then double that number. Push yourself to be creative and find new ways. You will be handsomely rewarded if you do.

When I first did this exercise, I shot for fifteen different ways to get what I wanted and ended up doubling that number!

If you're still having trouble, try this technique: Draw a line on a piece of paper like the one you see in Figure A on page 78. The objective is to shift your focus from the challenge to the solution. Your situation at present is A. This could represent the place where you currently are in your life, knowing that you have a goal you want to reach—or rather, knowing that you don't want to stay where you are. It could also represent a problem or challenge you must overcome in this moment and you are not sure how to do it. You've been thinking about it and are having difficulty coming up with a solution. First I will explain the theory of the diagram in Figure A; then we will look at a practical example.

The Power of Asking Yourself Good Questions

When you find yourself in a difficult situation or are faced with a seemingly insurmountable obstacle, identify what the obstacles are, but then immediately shift your focus to the solution. This is something else that Tony Robbins talks about in his book *Awaken the Giant Within*. He talks about the power of asking good questions—to yourself. It's important to know how to talk to yourself if you want good results, to understand the different types of questions to ask yourself, and the power that they can have on the results you get.

Questions have the power to change your focus immediately, to put you in another state of mind, to make you think. When we are asked a question, whether we decide to answer or not, we still think about a possible answer. This happens whether someone else asks a question or whether we ask ourselves. For example, I might begin the writing part of this book on the subject of the importance of goal-setting as follows, because I really want you to think about what I am saying:

- Can you imagine what your life would be like if you had never had any goals to reach?

- How do you think your life would be?

- But of course you do have goals. Don't you? What are they?

- Have you ever had any difficulty reaching objectives that you set for yourself, or has it always gone smoothly and without any unexpected obstacles? If so, when was that? Do you remember?

- If you could do it over again, what would you do differently?

- Have you always known exactly how to plan effectively for your goals?

- Have you always been 100 percent disciplined to follow your plan? If not, why?

- Do you think your plans were specific enough or could they have been more specific?

- If you had a proven method to help you effectively plan and execute anything in your life, how would that make you feel?

With each one of those questions, did you find yourself answering some or all of them in your head? That's the way our brains work. So what does that have to do with solving problems? A lot! When we find ourselves in a rut and are having difficulty figuring out what to do, we must ask ourselves questions. But you must ask yourself the right questions; positive questions that will help you shift your focus to help you find a positive outcome.

There are two types of questions: positive and negative. Negative questions keep you immersed in and focused on the problem. Positive questions are those that shift your focus, bringing you outside the crux of the problem. Here are some examples:

Empowering Questions and Language	Hindering Questions & Bad Language
• How can I get out of this situation?	• Why does this always happen to me?
• How can I turn this situation around for the positive?	• How come no one else has to go through this?
• What can I do that I haven't done already to better the situation?	• I'll never be able to get out of this mess.
• How can I turn this negative into a position of strength?	• I might as well go and tell her that I won't be able to make it.
• How many ways are there to get what I want?	• Why did she give me that part to prepare? I'll never have time to prepare that.
• Am I doing everything I can to resolve this situation?	• That's way too much. I'll never be able to handle that.
• What resources do I have in my possession—physical, mental, or otherwise that I could use to create a positive outcome?	• The only people who get out of situations like this have luck on their side or know the right people.
• What else could I be doing that I haven't yet tried?	• How come I always get myself into situations like this?
• Who could I ask?	• Will I ever really get what I want?
• Who could give me advice or steer me in the right direction?	• Am I destined to always be in positions like this?

That's what the following diagram is all about. First I'll explain it in general terms and then we'll apply a practical example.

You have a challenge, an obstacle to overcome, sometimes known as a *problem* (a word I don't like to use). This is where you begin at position A on the diagram on page 78 below. If we stay there with our current thought process, it will be difficult to find a solution. So we have to move away from position A. In situations like this, some people simply stay there, because they don't know what to do. Sometimes it is difficult to see a way out. How do we move away so that we don't just focus on the problem, but rather on a possible solution?

Go back to a time before this challenge presented itself, say three months, six months, or more ago. That's where position B is. Now start asking some good questions.

The First Alternative

Questions to ask yourself in position B:

- What were things like three months ago, before I had this issue to deal with?
- How was I behaving? What was the environment like?
- Who were the key players back then, or who were the people helping me who are no longer in the picture?
- What did I do correctly back then that I'm not doing now?
- What changed and why did it change?
- What would it take to get that back again?
- How can I re-create that same situation to overcome this obstacle and improve my position now?
- What would it take to do that?
- How do I feel emotionally, knowing that everything is running smoothly?

This approach may or may not be very effective for you, because the challenge that you face might be a new situation for you altogether. So what do you do? You have three more alternatives. Let's move to a point some time in the future, imagining that you have already resolved your issue. It could be several months or even a year or two down the road. This would be position C on the diagram. Now ask yourself questions that help you shift your focus to a point in time when you have already resolved the issue.

The Second Alternative

First visualize what it would be like to resolve the situation. In other words, visualize what success is. Visualize it in its smallest detail. If you have ever done any sensory work, it is very similar to this. You must imagine being in that situation in which your problem has been solved. Use all five senses. Actually see the steps you took to resolve the issue. What did you do exactly? Questions to ask yourself while at position C:

- What is the environment like now that I have resolved the situation?
- What changed?
- What did I do or what actions did I take to overcome this obstacle?
- Who helped me do it?

- How long did it take for me to do it?

- How did I create this ideal situation?

- How am I behaving differently now with respect to how I was before I solved the issue?

- How do I feel now emotionally that I have overcome this adversity?

- Would I be able to help someone else do the same thing? Do I really know how I did it?

- What steps did I take to resolve the situation?

The Third and Fourth Alternatives

Still don't have all the answers you need? You still have two other alternatives: Positions D1 and D2. Position D is someone or something that might have the answer for you or at least be able to guide you in the right direction. If position D is a person, it's someone who probably knows how to resolve the situation. It could be someone who has been through a similar ordeal, who has had to overcome the same obstacle at some point in his/her life or career. Or it could be that that person has been so efficient at managing his/her own affairs that they never had this issue to deal with. Position D1 is trying to put yourself in that person's shoes without having to ask him/her for advice. It is trying to figure out, by asking yourself good questions, what that person would do if he/she were in your shoes. Position D2 is when you actually go to that person and ask for advice, which might be a last resort, depending on which way you choose to use this technique. Go ask that person!

Why didn't I suggest that first? Because there is no specific order to move in. I personally prefer the way I showed you, because it helps you grow. It helps you think for yourself first. You will find that this method can be applied to just about any situation in which you find yourself stuck without an immediate answer. At least one of the positions should work for you to help you find alternatives.

If you need more help and coaching I can suggest other resources. First in New York: www.jolten.com : offers seminars, courses on an array of subjects to aid both companies and individuals achieve extraordinary results. You could also head over to www.actingcareerstartup.com. Another resource which helps actors and business people achieve results is www.successissweetest.com Janice Hoffman is a career and life-style coach. The Ward Studio of acting also offers an excellent career-mentoring program. For a further, excellent and detailed guide and journal with day to day tips, record-keeping forms and really all that an actor needs to manage "the business" is Leslie Becker's best-selling book, 'The Organized Actor'. Leslie is an actress with many years of experience, who has been sharing her knowledge and experience with actors in her book for over a decade. The book and other resources including seminars and personal coaching can be found on her website www.organizedactor.com. Still another excellent place to go for coaching is to Brian O'Neil's website at www.actingasabusiness.com. Brian is one of the most recognized experts in the industry when it comes to how to get work as an actor. Here are some questions you could ask yourself in position 'D1', which is to try and put yourself in his/her shoes and to imagine how that person would resolve things before you even physically go to the person, which would be position 'D2' to ask for help:

- If I were D, what would I do to resolve this situation?
- As D, why have I never had this issue to deal with?
- What actions have I taken to successfully avoid that situation?
- What would D do to help someone like me?
- How does D feel emotionally about the fact that he/she has never had this issue to deal with?
- How will I be able to ensure that something like that never happens to me?
- What am I doing to be successful in that regard?

D1 ● D2

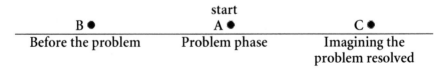

start

B ●   A ●   C ●
Before the problem   Problem phase   Imagining the
                                         problem resolved

Fig A.

You can apply this technique to just about any situation. For example, let's say that an actor has had an agent for a year, but the agent hasn't really done very much for her. She continues to look in *Backstage* to see casting notices that she feel's she's right for or to go to *Actors' Access* or other casting websites and send in her material for auditions. She has a few industry contacts, but all in all she's not getting very good results. She goes on about one to two auditions a week and continues to work her part-time job as a waitress. When she can get the money together, she'll take some classes. She'd like to take more, but she just can't afford it. They're too expensive. She's frustrated and disappointed. What should she do?

She could stay in position A and feel sorry for herself, but we know that wouldn't help. Going back in time to position B won't be very much help, because she has never experienced things going really well. But she could start to ask herself questions such as:

- What will I be doing in six months to ensure I get a lot of auditions?
- What will I need to do in order to ensure my agent sends me out on as many auditions as possible?
- What methods can I adopt to ensure that I will be noticed?
- How can I promote myself, and position myself for success in six months' time?
- Where will I be going to school?
- Where will I get the money to go to school?
- Which technique will help me to best express my artistic potential?
- How will I find out?
- How will I overcome my weaknesses?
- What agency will be best for me?
- How will I find out?
- What resources do I already have (financial, intellectual, material, etc.) that I can use to help me get what I want?

She must move forward and go to position C, asking herself good questions that shift her focus to getting some results instead of concentrating on the challenge she must overcome (which keeps her immersed in the present situation). In order to go to position C, though, she must have a clear idea of what she wants the situation to look like. She must imagine it in its smallest detail and then look back to today. She must be able to visualize what things will be like when she is going out on more auditions and booking work. Some other questions she might ask herself are:

- What am I doing to promote myself?
- What types of auditions am I going on now?
- Who is helping me get those auditions?
- Who am I auditioning for?
- What types of shows, programs, films?
- How is my confidence level since I've started going out and auditioning much more often?
- What kinds of classes am I taking now?
- Where am I studying? What school?
- What technique am I studying?
- Which technique helps me get the best results?
- How much does it cost?
- Where am I getting the money?
- What does my work situation look like?
- Why don't I have to worry anymore about getting off work for the increased number of auditions that I now have?
- How much more time do I devote to my craft than I used to, and what has changed to make all this possible?
- Who helped me get to this point?
- Who are my friends?
- Can they give me something that will help me get where I want to go?

Maybe she doesn't have all the answers or maybe she simply needs some help in organizing her thoughts and needs a mentor. She should think of someone who is already well established as an actor (or performer); someone who is working regularly or constantly auditioning and getting work; someone who seems to always be busy promoting herself/himself; someone who is experienced and who knows the ropes; and maybe someone who is a similar type. In any case, it must be someone who is getting good results. Instead of a person it could be a resource, Web site, book, magazine—anything.

This might sound like very basic information, but I know for a fact that many artists do not do these very simple things. That is why I am dedicating this book to a group of people who I know would appreciate a structured approach to problem solving.

Now, after having tried positions B and C, she has moved on to position D. She can first ask herself what person in position D would do. For example:

- How does D get so many auditions?
- How did she get such a good agent?
- Does the agent do all the work in finding the auditions?
- What activities does she do to promote herself that I'm not doing?
- What trade papers does she read?
- What online organizations is she a member of?
- What else does she do to keep abreast of industry trends?
- How is she making and keeping contacts?
- What do her headshots look like?
- What does she have on her résumé? How is it formatted?
- Does she use picture postcards?
- Does she go to any forums to make industry contacts?
- Does she have a mentor or a coach who helps her?
- How does she afford to take classes all the time?
- With all those auditions, how does she get off work?
- When does she have time to prepare for her auditions? Rehearsals?
- How does she prepare?
- Where is she studying? What school does she go to?
- What technique works for her and why?
- Why did she choose that one as opposed to another?
- What are some of the lessons that she has learned along the way that I might be able to learn from?

Now, depending on the situation that our young actor is in, she might be able to find out some of these things right away. She may or may not need to know the answers to all the questions. If she needs to know more, she'll have to ask someone or think of some other resources that can help her. She also needs to identify her focus and goal so that she can ask pointed and intelligent questions that will help her reach her goal. What's important is to move out of the problem mode and into the solution mode.

Don't stop until you get what you want!

Big Ideas

This section is dedicated to one of my greatest teachers, who probably hasn't a clue how I feel about him, because I never told him. I always respected him. He comes from my days in Nike, and his name is Gary De Stefano, a corporate vice president. About ten years ago when I was the European director of sales training and development out of Nike's European HQ in the Netherlands, I was at a meeting in California. Gary had brought all the country sales directors together for a global meeting, where we decided collectively on global strategies to implement. Whenever we had these meetings, there was always a brainstorming session that Gary entitled "Big Ideas," where we would come up with ideas on how to grow the business.

It is important to know what the true meaning of brainstorming is. Brainstorming is a process during which you throw out any and all ideas that could help solve a certain challenge or issue that one might have. During this process, there are no bad, stupid, ridiculous ideas. There are no unrealistic or unachievable ideas. Every idea counts. These ideas are all to be considered valid. There is then a second phase in which the feasibility and appropriateness is weighed and it is decided whether it will be worth the effort necessary to make it happen.

Those sessions helped mold me into what I am now. We were challenged to come up with something innovative, something different, and, most of all, something big! No idea was too big; after all, we were just brainstorming. I loved those sessions. Whenever I talk today about innovation and doing things differently, I get excited at the prospect of trying to create something that no one else has. It is not always easy coming up with new things, but the more you weave this thinking into your everyday life, the easier it becomes.

If you have been studying acting for a while, then you have certainly worked on your choices at sometime or another. I remember classes in which we were challenged to come up with new choices every other class. Difficult! Our creativity as actors is continuously challenged. A great teacher once said, "An actor's talent lies in his choices."

What big ideas do you have to further your career?

Be Your Own Person

Wanting to be my own man is something that is in my blood. I remember back in 1992 when Michael Jordan came to Germany for a promotional tour with Nike. The week before he arrived, the sports promotion manager, who normally would have been Michael's personal escort, broke his leg and could no longer take on that task. He asked me if I had anything important planned for that next week because he needed someone to escort Michael around for the week and to be his interpreter. I struck a pensive look and rubbed my chin (one of my first acting performances) and told him I would have to think about it. After just one second, I said yes! What an opportunity—to spend a week with one of the greatest sports legends ever! I did ask, however, if I was to be Michael's personal escort and accompany him everywhere he went, or if I was meant to be just his driver and stay outside and wax the car while he was doing whatever he had to do. I told the manager that, being the only black person in Nike Germany at the time, I didn't think Michael would appreciate me being his chauffeur, not to mention the fact that I wouldn't have wanted to do that and I would not have done it. I was assured that I was to be his personal escort and accompany him on this tour. The company gave me a BMW 850 for the week and it was me; Michael; and Howard White, Michael's personal Nike sports marketing representative.

Nike had had T-shirts made up with Michael Jordan's picture and gave them to all the staff to wear. I refused to wear it. I talked to Michael about it. I told him that for me he was the greatest basketball player of all times and that I admire him as an individual, but I couldn't wear a shirt with his or anyone else's picture on it because I don't idolize anyone. I want to be and remain Anthony Lee Smith. He cracked a little smile and told me that he respected that and that he perfectly understood. He proceeded to tell me that he was often bothered by adult autograph seekers, because he couldn't understand why an adult would want another's autograph. He couldn't understand what could be so great about another adult that would make someone want his signature. He told me that he could identify with my thinking.

Why is being your own person so important? Because sometimes going after what you want can be a long and lonely road. Of all the people around you on a continuous basis, you might be the only one who believes in what you are striving for. It might be difficult to find someone who shares your way of thinking and your vision. You might often run into people who will try and talk you out of what you are trying to achieve. They will try hard at times to rain on your parade. In moments like these, you will be put to the test to see how much you really believe in your goals and how much you really want to achieve them. Are you really your own person?

CHAPTER 8

Stay Ahead of the Game!

Lessons in Innovation

I started working for Nike back in 1990 as a technical consultant. As you have probably gathered by now, it was not only a job, but also a mission, a great experience that taught me a lot.

I was responsible for going to our existing retail customers and holding clinics and seminars to inform store owners and their salespeople about the technical aspects of Nike footwear and apparel so that when their customers came into their stores, they would know how to advise them more effectively as to what kind of Nike shoes or apparel would be right for them. In those early days, I heard the Nike story many times from the company historian Nelson Farris. He was mesmerizing when he told the story. He was there and lived it every step of the way. Aside from all the technical information we gave our customers, we also often told the story about how Nike came to be, about Phil Knight, the business graduate student and his track coach, Bill Bowerman, and how they wanted to make shoes for runners. About how Bowerman made the first outsoles for his runners by hand by baking the rubber in a waffle iron to give them the traction runners needed to perform better and about how innovation became one of the company's core values.

We also learned about how Frank Rudy, an engineer, had taken his then-absurdly innovative invention of a cushioning system to others in the traditional and sports shoe markets (including some of Nike's competitors) and was turned down numerous times until Knight and Bowerman gave him the nod and he was in. They bought his system and called it Nike Air, a unique mix of gas whose molecules were so large that it was impossible for them to escape the membrane around them; thus the cushioning system lasted for the life of the shoe.

Breakthrough Innovation

In 1979, the very first Nike Air shoe, Air Tailwind, was introduced into the market; the shoe's heel area consisted of Nike Air, something previously unheard of. There was much criticism from industry experts. Many said that it wasn't a good idea, that it was just a marketing gimmick, that the air sole would break, that it was unstable. The list of negative comments went on. There were, however, many positive things said. It was different and there was much excitement among runners. It was innovative, and, most importantly, it was something that no other company had.

At the same time the Air Tailwind hit the market, according to the book *Nike and the Men Who Played There,* "a Brooks spokesman said his shoe company was coming out with an air-cushioned shoe 'very soon' that would have its own pump to replenish the air when it diminished." Other competitors condemned this new technology or tried to downplay it. When you're on top, people will try and shoot you down or copy you. You have to be ready for that. It's part of the game of life.

Nike's founders continued over the years to build more shoes while continuously evolving the revolutionary cushioning system. They brought more innovation into the footwear line as well as into the apparel and accessories they produced. They invested huge amounts of money in research and development to stay ahead of the game. The company invested more and more money in the endorsement of top athlete like Steve Prefontaine, John McEnroe, Alberto Salazar, Michael Jordan, Moses Malone, Andre Agassi, Michael Johnson, Dan Fouts, and many others, which at the time was another revolutionary idea. All this helped Nike's founders grow it into a $14 billion company.

Innovation is what keeps companies like Nike solid, profitable, and stable, and it is what gives them longevity.

Does it sound like I'm touting the Nike horn? Well, maybe I am a little, because it has had its effect on me and still does. It's a great place to work, but I left because, as Steven Covey said in his book *The 7 Habits of Highly Effective People,* "It's easy to say no when there's a deeper yes burning within."

One of the great lessons I learned from working there was that if we want to be successful, be noticed, stand out, then we must innovate and do something different. If we keep doing what we've been doing, we will keep getting what we get. One day that might not be good enough anymore, so those of us who really want to be successful in this business of performing, in which the competition is so great, we must be innovative, to think of different ways to stand out from the crowd. And we must do it continuously.

Like I said before, you gotta think big! Huge ideas. Winning ideas. Fantastic ideas. Incredible ideas. Think about the adjectives you use to describe your projects and plans. These are the words I use: *Gigantic. Phenomenal. Unbelievable. Smashing. Awesome.* If you come from a different generation, you might use phrases such as "That's tight!" "Fly!" "The shit!" "That's on!" Whatever you use to describe your plans, make sure you use words that mean big things. It will change the perception, even for you!

Check out what this meant for Knight and Bowerman and what they brought to the market over the years. The following excerpt is taken from www.nikebiz.com.

Nike Timeline:

1971
Frustrated with the inability to secure loans at local banks, Knight finds a new method of creative financing. Through the Bank of Tokyo, a trading company called Nissho Iwai introduces BRS to import letters of credit and lays the foundation for future rapid growth.

1974
The WAFFLE TRAINER is introduced featuring Coach Bowerman's famous Waffle outsole. It quickly becomes the best-selling training shoe in the country.

1978
Blue Ribbon Sports officially changes its name to Nike, Inc. on May 30. Tennis great John McEnroe signs a deal with the company. Nike recognizes itself in McEnroe's colorful character and feisty personality.

1979
After a very limited release in Hawaii timed to the Honolulu Marathon on November 30, 1978, Nike introduces the TAILWIND, the first running shoe with Nike Air, the technologically advanced, patented Air-Sole cushioning system.

1985
Chicago Bulls basketball rookie Michael Jordan endorses a Nike line of AIR JORDAN court shoes and specialized apparel.

1987
The Air Max shoe, giving athletes their first look at Nike-AIR cushioning, is introduced by the controversial "Revolution" ad campaign.

1988

Just Do It ad—It became both universal and intensely personal. It spoke of sports. It invited dreams. It was a call to action, a refusal to hear excuses, and a license to be eccentric, courageous and exceptional. It was Nike. This campaign is now ensconced in the Americana exhibit at the Smithsonian National Museum—it truly became part of America's history.

1988

Nike breaks new ground with the acquisition of Cole Haan. The American luxury brand, Cole Haan, makes men's and women's footwear, accessories and outerwear focusing on craftsmanship, design innovation and character.

1990

The first Niketown opens in Portland, Oregon. The store invents pure sports retail with 23,095 sq. ft. of athlete-driven award-winning design.

1993

Nike introduces an innovative sustainability program, Reuse-A-Shoe which collects athletic shoes, separates and grinds them up into Nike Grind which is used in the making of athletic courts, tracks and fields.

1995

Nike enters the hockey arena with the acquisition of Canstar Sports Inc., which includes Bauer, and introduces its first skate, Air Eccel Elite. All Canstar brands were later consolidated under the Bauer brand name (1998).

2000

Nike designs uniforms for over 2,000 athletes at the Sydney Games for 25 sports. The Games give Nike the perfect opportunity to introduce high-performance, innovative products to the world, including revealing the lightest track spike ever made, the aerodynamic and thermo-regulatory Swift Suit, the recyclable Marathon Singlet and a new standard in responsive cushioning systems called Nike Shox.

2002

NikeGO launches—nationwide community program to increase physical activity in American youth.

2003
Converse Inc. joins the growing Nike portfolio.

2004
In August, Nike created the Exeter Brands Group, a wholly owned subsidiary, dedicated to building athletic footwear and apparel brands for the value retail channel.

2004
Nike acquired the Official Starter Properties LLC and Official Starter LLC which are the sole owners and licensors of the Starter, Team Starter and Asphalt brand names as well as master licensee of the Shaq and Dunkman brands, a line of athletic apparel, footwear and accessory products for the value retail channel.

And those are just a few of the innovations over the years. There's much more to that story. As you can see, over the years, there was always something new they were coming up with. Always. Each time they came out with a new shoe, the competitors copied them. Each and every time. If you stay where you are, competitors catch up to you; then you're just like everyone else, unless you change and make everyone else play catch-up. It makes you more interesting. It makes people pay attention to you. You lead the market; the market doesn't lead you. I saw prototypes of the Shox shoe, for example, ten years ago, while it was still in the development stage. The shoe came out five years later, and by the time I had seen the prototypes, it had already been being researched for five years.

So what else did I learn from that? It takes effort and time and much thought and innovation to stay ahead of the game and of your competitors. I learned that if I have to think about how to win out over my competition, I first have to know who it is, which I will talk about shortly. Secondly, I have to know who my customers are. Thirdly, I have to know what they want. And that is how I came up with the idea for a way to launch a new project, of which this book is just a part. I realized that there have to be different ways of learning the business myself, meeting industry professionals, and doing all the homework necessary to be successful. I had to create something different, not just in this project, but in everything I do.

CHAPTER 9

Creating the Necessary Motivation:
Burn the Ships!

In the year 1519, Hernando Cortez set out to conquer the Aztecs. It was common knowledge that the Aztecs were a formidable opponent and that they would be difficult to conquer. When he set out, Cortez didn't have nearly the number of men, horses, or cannons that one would think necessary to match such an enemy. Many among his men were afraid that they would be massacred, for the adversary was mighty, had a reputation for wreaking havoc, and had much fighting experience. Cortez overheard some of his men expressing their concern that they might not return home. Upon their landing, he ordered his ships be burned; while watching, his men listened to him say that now they have no choice: "Either we will win or we will all perish." They were victorious.

Have you ever heard the saying, "Hungry dogs hunt better" or, "A tiger hunts best when he's hungry"? To be really motivated, you have to be hungry, really want it, because you will be driven and determined and unstoppable! When I decided to embark on this mission, I burnt my ships. There's no turning back now. I must go forward. I must succeed.

This brings me to how you keep alive the process of going after what you want. This is why it is important to do the groundwork at the beginning to figure out what it really is that you want. If you want to be an actor, for example, yet can't seem to get motivated to make your rounds, read the trade papers, make contacts, go to classes, build your contacts, and so on, then this could be a sign that something isn't right. You need motivation! If you don't have adequate motivation, try making a list of all the reasons why your goal is so important to you, why you must achieve it. Don't stop at one or two reasons. Having a lot of reasons for doing what it is you want to do helps to increase your motivation. The more good and strong reasons you have, the stronger your motivation will be. Think! You'll surprise yourself.

Why I want to _____

1. _____   6. _____

2. _____   7. _____

3. _____   8. _____

4. _____   9. _____

5. _____   10. _____

Now that you have ten reasons listed, I challenge you to double that number with ten more good and valid reasons!

For me, the following sentence continues to motivate me each and every single day.

So, I can say that this book and the rest of this project that I have created, gives me that chance that I have created for myself to be able to practice my acting on video, write, help others, promote myself and others, rediscover parts of myself, learn about the industry, create opportunities for myself and for others, put myself on the line, have fun, have the flexibility I need to concentrate on developing my craft, spend time with my son, learn, make a difference, tell stories, dream, have an audience, perform, innovate, express myself, share, challenge myself, study, blow off steam, develop my creativity, explore, be myself, grow, give, be humble, positively affect people's lives, meet the right people to further my career, audition, reach my goals, make money, teach my son how to make money, believe that what I want is possible, lead, be an example, work, and prepare myself for an inevitable evolution and creation of my own timeline of innovation. Altogether there are forty things on that list of mine. I always think of at least a couple of those things, which always reminds me of the importance of what I am doing. If I'm not thinking about one thing, I'm thinking about another. Later I will talk about finding the motivation to do what you want to do.

Turn the Clock Ahead

How many times have you heard someone say, "If I only knew then what I know now, I would have…" Maybe you've even said that yourself. I know I have. Well, when I think about the course of my life, I know that I could have done many things better. I can remember things that my parents told me and

I didn't want to listen. When I think back about some of those things, I wish I would have paid attention. For example, if I had listened to my parents about saving money, I would be a lot better off now. If I had followed some of my colleagues' advice on investing in certain stocks, I would have a larger nest egg than I have now. If I had taken better care of myself and watched my eating habits, I wouldn't have had problems with my stomach and had to deprive myself of certain foods for a good part of my life. If, if, if…We can't go back. We can only go forward.

For a couple of years now, I've been really aware of senior citizens. I've been observing how slowly they move, which is normal. I see how many have physical difficulty moving, how some even need to be helped, because they can't care for themselves. I've seen that senior citizens aren't the only ones who have these challenges. There are many people even younger who are physically challenged as well. Some of these people I have grown up with. Some of these people I have known for years. The thing that strikes me is that some I remember when they were younger and very vibrant, mobile, agile, young, spunky, full of energy! When I see them now, I hardly know them anymore. They've changed so much.

When I get older, I want to still be fit. When I am older, I want to move and be alive and get around on my own. I want to live to be over 100 years old, and when I am that age, I want to be active, do sports, and have sex regularly. I want to be of sound mind, read, and do all the things I do now. That is my wish for myself. If you don't believe that that is possible, then it never will be! If I start educating myself about problems older men have, I can start now to at least try and avoid those challenges.

A couple of years ago, I went to a seminar that was, in part, spiritual in nature. The seminar leader was a very knowledgeable person named Roy Martina, a Dutchman who has written over fifty books and who also, when he was younger, was the European karate champion in his weight class for several years in a row. He did a session on the importance of aligning the conscious with the subconscious. Sometimes we sabotage ourselves, because on the conscious level we want certain things, but on the subconscious level we do things to make our conscious desires more difficult, as the subconscious has its own ideas about what we should have. One thing about this particular session that really intrigued me was what he said about age and dying. He said that our subconscious already has programmed in an age at which we think we will die and that all of our actions and ways of being, eating, taking care of ourselves, our habits and the way we see the world are all in line with the date when we think we will die.

I'm not an expert on this and I'm not trying to sell you this idea, but it did make me think.

Now I look at those older folks and think about myself. I just do it automatically. Are we guaranteed to make it to senior citizen age? Of course we are not. I think about those senior citizens, especially the ones who are vibrant and of sound mind, who are mobile and self-sufficient, and I want to be like that! So what do I do? I start now to manage my own destiny as much as possible. I start now to watch what I eat, to exercise, to inform myself as to what I can do to ensure that I will be the way I want to be when I get older. I can't control everything, but maybe there is one thing I can control that will save my life or enable me to live a certain way. If I don't do these things, it simply means that they were not important enough to me, so I will accept the consequences whatever they will be and whenever they come.

All this puts a flame under my butt! It makes me want to move *now*, because no one can guarantee that I will be here tomorrow. I don't want my dreams to die with me. I want them to live on after I am gone. Sound tragic? Think about how tragic it would be if you didn't do all the things you want to do before you make a departure from this earth!

This is one of the things that drives *me*, and for *me* it's working, because there isn't a day that I don't wake up thinking about where I am on my goals and what I want to leave as a legacy. Not one day.

Find out what drives you. Put the flame under your butt and get a move on. Time is passing you by! If you have to, turn your clock ahead and ask yourself how your life will be when you are older and if you will have accomplished all the things you wanted to before you go on to your next life.

If you need help finding motivation or getting stimulated to achieve greater results than the ones you are getting now, I can highly recommend one of the teachers who is excellent at helping actors maximize their potential. His name is Bernard Hiller, and he is a Hollywood acting coach. You can find him at www.bernardhiller.com. If you think you are motivated and are doing a lot now to further your career, wait till you take one of his classes. He is a master at showing actors how they could be doing more and helping you find the necessary motivation to do it.

I want to make sure I do as many of the things that I want to on this earth before I meet my maker! How about you? The question is, if we continue at the rate we are doing things right now, will we get all those things done? Where were you five years ago? What significant achievements have you made since then? Did you do everything you could have in these last five years? If you continue to do what you are doing, where will you be five years from now? Will that be good enough for you? Get motivated and do what you need to do. Now!

Ya Gotta Love It!

Like my football coach used to tell us when we were in summer camp, practicing in the sweltering heat, "Men, ya gotta love it! When it's too hot for the other teams, it'll be just right for us!" Toward the end of the season in mid-November, he used to say, "When it's too cold for the other teams, it'll be just right for us!" You have to have that mentality. If doing what's necessary is a drag and a sacrifice, then why do it at all?

I saw an article in a trade paper recently that answered the question, "How do I know that acting is right for me?" The answer given was disputable, but I tend to agree with it: "If you have to ask that question, then the answer is that acting is probably not right for you." When you are driven and motivated, your heart tells you. Your gut tells you that it is right. You have a list of things that tell you this is what's right for you. Just like my project. I have listed over thirty different reasons why this is right for me and I love it. It makes me feel good, because no matter what I do around that project, I'm doing something that I love to do. It's a great feeling.

Joshua's Learning Early

My son, Joshua, is becoming a very good soccer player. Here in Italy, folks are wild about the game, just as they are in most parts of the world. He's only ten years old, but he already has a clear idea of what he wants to do, or so he says, just like many kids his age. He told me many times that he wants to be the best soccer player in the world. Of course, at ten years of age, he doesn't really understand the scope of his statement, but the determination is there. The passion is there. He doesn't leave one room of the house without a sponge soccer ball on his foot. He doesn't brush his teeth or set the table or do his homework without his ball. He practices his kicks and new moves, he imagines situations, and he commentates his own little imaginary games, in which of course he is the star. During his games, he can be counted on to contribute anywhere between one and three goals or assists a game on the average. He's got great technical skills and a sense for the ball that many kids develop at a later age. While I'm proud of him, I'm not naïve enough to realize that with him being a kid, his passion could change and soccer will be history, especially if he's not coached. But there's another reason why I'm telling you this little story.

Just as I was when I was his age, he is just plain skinny. Healthy and energetic, but skinny. He must gain some weight and get a bit stronger. He's a good fifteen to twenty pounds lighter than average for his age. He's not a big eater, but he's got to eat more. When he's older, he'll be able to work out with the weights, but he's too young for that now. I've been coaching him off the field. We look at films of his games and look at what he does well and what he could improve on. We look at certain plays and rewind them if necessary to get another look. It's all about learning from experience in order to get better, a technique I learned while playing high school and college football.

I've been coaching him on the fact that to be a great player, he must be good at different aspects of his game. For example, he's already good at kicking and handling the ball with his left foot, but he's got to work on his right. We talked about how he must improve his ball-handling skills, stopping, controlling, pushing the ball up the field; working on endurance, and whatever else is necessary. We talked about how important it is for him to eat what's on his plate, because he needs to get bigger and stronger. He tells me that at school he doesn't eat, because the food isn't good or he only eats what he likes.

After our discussions, he understands that if it is really important to him to become the greatest soccer player in the world, he must begin now and work on all aspects of his game and that eating to get bigger and stronger is part of the whole picture. I have also tried to instill in him that when something is really important, he must find time to do whatever is necessary to make sure he gets what he want. Make sacrifices. Do your exercises. Eat even what you don't like. He's learning, but of course he has a long way to go. And he is not alone in this. He will have help.

I told him of how Michael Jordan improved his game. Once his adversaries knew that he was always on the prowl for a slam-dunk, they got wise and blocked him out of the middle. So what did he do? He worked on his outside game. He became a good three-point shooter. He could dribble well to both sides. He would stay after practice to work on improving his game. He improved the talent he already had and sharpened it even more. He then became a threat from anywhere on the court.

Now, Joshua is only ten years old, but we are adults, old enough to know that if we really want to do something, we need to stop making excuses for ourselves! While I believe in the idea that repetition helps to drive home concepts, that if we hear them just once or twice, they will have no effect on us, we should at least have the courage to look ourselves in the mirror and tell ourselves the truth and instead of saying things like, "I didn't have time" or "I was too busy." Instead we should simply say, "It just wasn't that important to me at that time." It's being real. It's being honest with ourselves about who we are and about what we really want.

Pep Talks!

Do you ever talk to yourself sometimes when you're alone? I do. I spend a lot of time alone during the day when I'm preparing for my courses and seminars and doing office work, and I talk to myself every day. It just happens. I'm so psyched and driven about what I'm doing and about the prospects for the future and for success that I get excited! I sometimes stop what I'm doing, whether thinking about a new seminar or course I want to offer or about a book project. I stand up and turn to an imaginary audience that could be just a few people or a full auditorium. I speak to them just as I would in real life.

Am I saying you should do the same thing? No. But you should do what works for you. For me, this is part of the whole process. It is part of the motivation that I have created inside myself, and it comes out and manifests itself in this way. When I do go up in front of an audience, I am much more convincing. Remember when we talked about how sometimes when you tell someone your goal, they might not find you very convincing? Well, talking to yourself, even while looking in the mirror, is a good way to see just how convinced you are about what you are saying. Even without looking in the mirror, though, especially if you are an actor or performer, you *know* whether you are convinced about whether you can be successful or not. The people you talk to about it will see it. The most important thing, however, is that you feel it! If you do, then you don't have to worry about what others think.

I tell myself numerous times each day that I must make it, that I must be successful in my endeavor, that I will definitely be successful. I will write my book and distribute it. I will write that article, involve that person in my business, create that seminar, develop that project, and so on. I tell myself these things constantly and test my level of conviction when I say them. Then I periodically mention these things to my son. I tell him, "Joshua, guess what, son?" He says, "What?" I say, "I'm gonna make it!" He rolls his eyes and tells me that I already told him that. So I run over to him and give him a hug and a kiss and tell him that I just wanted him to know again!

So, after having done all this groundwork, you have to make a decision that will change your life forever. Are you going to commit?

Commit 110 Percent...

In a workshop with a noted casting director, we were being enlightened as to the dos and don'ts of auditioning. One of the things she told us was that some questions are okay to ask the casting director about the scene you are reading for when you go in for the audition. On the other hand, she told us that, the one question she doesn't like to hear is one regarding the relationship between the two people in the scene. (For example: Are they husband and wife? Did something happen to her to make her speak that way to him?, etc.) Her advice was to determine for yourself the relationship between the two people, commit to it 100 percent, and do the read. We know that if we don't commit, it won't be a real performance.

This same principle applies to what we're doing here.

This is a great prelude to the planning process. You must start *now* to plan for what you want in the short, medium, and long terms.

Are you a procrastinator? Let me tell you what the true meaning of *procrastination* is. It is nothing more than the lack of motivation to do what you know you should, what you would like to do. It means that in that moment, you decide not to do it, that thing, whatever it is, isn't that important to you.

In Nike, there is a great sports culture. Practicing some kind of sport or doing fitness or training is encouraged. On the campus of the world headquarters, there are two huge gyms, several playing fields, and a running path that goes around the entire complex. There was a saying that was used as a slogan in one of the catalogues: "Either you ran today or you didn't." There are no excuses. Sometimes someone might say something like, "I got to bed late last night, so I didn't have time to get up and run before work. Or, I didn't have time today. We were in meetings all day." The fact is, whether you got to bed late or not, whether you had meetings all day or not, you could have found time if you wanted to. If something is that important to you, you will get up thirty minutes early and run. So if you are having trouble moving your backside to get things done, then get yourself a healthy dose of motivation by trying what I suggest in the aforementioned text. You'll be glad you did!

...and Be a Go-Getter!

While discussing actors and artists, and the difficulties we face with career coach Janice Hoffman, I asked her for the profile of a typical student of hers and she told me about Dayton:

Dayton is thirty years old, educated, has a bachelors degree from a university, but instead of studying acting or theater, he majored in liberal arts, political science, although in his heart of hearts he's always wanted to be an actor.

He's come to New York and he's ravenous, really eager and pretty savvy when it comes to building relationships. He finds himself a flexible and decent-paying day job at a literary office. He's already leveraged this job by surrounding himself with people who are young, into pop culture and the trends of the city, nightlife and cultural events. He's a connector who's naturally curious and willing to work very hard.

Let's say that one of Dayton's biggest assets at this point is that he really "gets" that he's lagging behind as a competitive actor and he instinctively knows he needs to put in longer hours than most, so he trains hard and is willing to sacrifice more. Dayton sets himself apart in this instance; even though he lacks experience, he is so driven and gets more done than any three people around him.

Another thing Dayton does is he gets out there. He takes in everything, reads, meets people and auditions for anything, and I mean anything. He's dedicated to learning and within one year, Dayton has gotten a small part in an off-Broadway show.

His fellow classmates at this stage might be technically better, but they don't have the internal game to venture outside the school environment. Dayton takes risks and is capable of learning from performance, from the audience, from the business of rejection, and his game is getting bigger. As he auditions, trains, rehearses, and performs, he starts to gain a competitive edge. He's very ambitious and could be classified as a guerilla marketer. He has an unconventional picture. In addition, he has started getting feedback form workshops and some actual reviews and has created some interesting and captivating cover letters using this material.

Dayton mainly markets through people. He always makes it his business to know who is doing what and then pursues them relentlessly. He studies continuously and takes classes and workshops with people who run theaters and with casting directors and other industry professionals, and he is very good at keeping in touch and following up with postcards. He has overall good business skills and is especially strong in the area of networking. Dayton's biggest assets are the solid industry relationships that he has been able to build. He's been cast in several major festivals through people who referred him from other things.

As things go, a friend of a friend tells him about an audition for a national tour. He's business ready, on point, and manages to sail through a very big audition. It's not unlike a Dayton-type actor to bypass some of the major obstacles that most actors encounter. He gets his first break by becoming an Equity member within two years of moving to NYC, not to mention that his new circle of friends and peers are all working actors. He is now getting more work on commercials as well as small roles on prime-time series.

Dayton has just become a professional actor. He's focused, disciplined, and he's no less in love with the craft than his classmates who never left the classroom.

Dayton is a typical profile of a New York actor who actually breaks into the business. Most of my clients are semiprofessional by the time I work with them, and I see this common thread among them.

Stay Positive!

Don't listen to all the waves of negativity around you! Have you ever told someone about a goal you had and had them just look at you trying to figure out if you're serious? What did your folks say when you said you wanted to become an artist? How many times have you expressed your ambitions to friends and had them tell you that you're crazy or that you'll never be able to do it or that it's difficult to do that?

Did you ever stop and think about why people say these things? There are several different reasons. One is that people don't always see things the same way you do. They don't have all the information that you do, so it is impossible for them to feel the same way about your goals. Another reason is because they want you to keep them company with the rest of the non-achievers and people who aren't successful or ambitious. Many of the people we tell our dreams, goals, and ambitions to have never done anything in your field, so they base their opinions and beliefs on what they know, have seen, and believe.

Sometimes it has to do with jealousy. This is common among actors and performers, even though it doesn't make sense especially when you consider that we are not all in competition with each other. You know what I'm talking about? The envy actors feel when someone else gets a part, or the reluctance actors feel when another actor who is doing well and who is strong and growing asks for information about an agent or another industry contact. People are resistant to give up this information for fear that person might make it before they do. Come on, people!

Oftentimes, people are envious of someone who isn't even in direct competition with them. That person would never even be up for the same role as you! Remember this: The more you give, the more you receive. If you help someone, it just might come back to you one day, even though I hope that is not the only reason you would want to help a fellow artist. Don't let that kind of attitude get the best of you. Stay positive and focused on your goals.

Don't let the negativity of others get to you! You can't listen to them. They will pull you down. You must have thick skin and have the courage to go the road alone if necessary. It can be very lonely. When you ask yourself what you are willing to do or sacrifice for your goal, loneliness is one of the things you must consider. You may not have anyone close to you who really understands what you are going through. There might not be anyone who can give you advice at midnight or at 2:00 a.m. if you need it, so, you must go it alone.

To keep the negative people out of your hair, let me tell you what you need. I saw the movie *The Incredibles* with my son. It's about a family that has super-human powers. The father is indestructible. The mother is super-elastic. The son has superhuman speed. And my favorite character, the daughter, Violet, has an indestructible bubble that she can place around herself, and nothing can get to her or harm her. *That's* what you need to do when you hear people telling you that you can't accomplish your goal! Put up your protective shield and don't let those negative comments affect you. How do you do that? You must be convinced more than anything else. You must back up your convictions with proof that you can do it. Not proof for them, but proof for yourself.

There will be some lowlifes who think they have the right to give you advice and tell you what they think you should be doing or that you will never make it or that it is too difficult or that others have tried and failed and blah, blah, blah. When I say *lowlife*, I mean someone with a losing mentality. You know, the people who are always negative no matter what you say; they always have some reason why it's not good or why it won't work. The kind who gives everyone else advice but doesn't have any goals or aspirations themselves. I do not permit these kinds of people to advise me, because they haven't done anything! At the most, they might say something that sparks an idea, but usually these people help fuel my desire even more to be successful. Like Will Smith said in one of his songs, "I take your insults and use them for fuel."

Do Your Homework!

The information and statistics that I discussed in the introduction to this book are also on the SAG, AFTRA, and EQUITY Web sites. You just have to know where to look. I was initially interested in getting the statistics for two reasons: One, any entrepreneur knows that before successfully launching into a new market or into one with which they are not familiar, they must first know something about it. Two, I was very curious to know who my competition is. When I first told people that I was going to become an actor, one of the first things they said (and still do today) is that there is a lot of competition. True. They said that I was competing against all the hundreds of thousands if not more than a million other actors in the United States alone. Not true! I'm a young, forty-six-year-old, Afro-American, light-skinned, physically fit, ethnically ambiguous-looking male. Based on my looks I could play a lawyer, doctor, businessman, detective between the age of thirty-eight to forty-eight. All the other actors out there are not in this same category. Does that mean that I still don't have a lot of competition? No. But the field is narrowed quite a bit.

Lessons from a Great Man

On January 15, 2007, Dr. Martin Luther King Jr., one of the greatest men in history, would have been seventy-eight years old. He dedicated his life to civil and human rights and is largely responsible for the way Americans live together today. He sought to ensure that all Americans, as stated in the Constitution, were treated equally. That was a tall task, especially in those times. All odds were against him. Guided by strong beliefs, not only of religious nature, but also of what was right and wrong, just and unjust in the United States of America, he was ultimately successful.

His clear vision of what he was striving for in the name of black America, his determination, strong communication skills, and his method were just some of the other things that helped him overcome the obstacles on the way to the victory he never lived to see.

He was a great man with a great vision, but he didn't know everything about how to achieve his goal. That is why he went to India in February of 1959 to visit Ghandi and study his methods of nonviolent protest.

"I Have a Dream"

Of his many great speeches, "I Have a Dream" is his most famous. He delivered it in front of the Lincoln Memorial in Washington, D.C., on August 28, 1963, before a crowd of some 250,000 people. He talked of his *vision* of how America should one day be, where "little black boys and little white girls would one day hold hands together." He communicated to his audience the America that he *imagined*.

On April 3, 1968, he gave another very memorable speech in which he seemed to be aware of the fact that he was in danger of being assassinated: "Some of you have talked to me about what some of those evil white men might do to me. I'm not worried about that now." He said that what was important was that after he was gone, we all continue the journey he started. In this speech, he spoke of having been to the mountaintop and how God let him see "the promised land" and how black people would get there with or without him. He stressed how important it was that black Americans continue on this journey for freedom. One day later, Martin Luther King Jr. was dead.

Aside from the fact that my family, like many others, were personally touched by the trials and tribulations of that era of our nation's history, I've always been inspired by Martin Luther King and by what he has taught us— not only about the strength of character, but also with regard to achieving greatness or even just simply achieving what one sets out to achieve.

It's time to act! I like thinking about what we can learn from a man like him; not just the human aspect, but also the stuff that it takes to achieve what one strives for. The same things that made him successful and overcome great odds in the fight for civil rights are the same principles that can help us in our every-day lives to achieve what we want:

- Clear vision of what we want the future to look like
- Desire
- Belief that it is possible
- Determination
- Planning
- Method
- Not trying to do everything alone
- Willingness to sacrifice
- Seeking out a mentor, someone who can help
- Sense of responsibility
- Preparing things for he who comes after you
- Giving
- Using unconventional methods
- Commitment to the cause

Do you have a dream? Do you have these qualities when it comes to the cause that you believe in? If you do, you will feel how powerful the energy is! Remember, there is a formula for success. If you don't have some of these qualities, it doesn't mean that you can't acquire them or learn them. It doesn't matter what you have or haven't done, what you have or have not achieved. You can still make progress and achieve more than you have up to this point in your life. That's what we're here for, right?

KEY FACTOR #3

Creation Of The Master Plan:
Ensuring Your Success

"If you fail to plan, you plan to fail."

anonymous

CHAPTER 10

The Master Plan

Do you have a plan or are you just waiting to see what happens?

I love that question. Is it logical to think that a person who knows what she wants, would want to do everything possible to increase her chances of getting it? I think so. And you?

In this section I will take you through the planning process so that you can have a greater probability of reaching your goals.

You've already worked on what it is you want and are starting to have an idea as to what your life's purpose is and how your acting career fits that scenario. Now it's time to set it in stone. You might need to go deeper into this process in order to further clarify what you want to do in life or to better identify your goal in the realm of acting (i.e., What kind of actor you would like to be and where you would like to reside—NY or LA? For example). Once you have a clear idea of what you want, are convinced that is the right thing for you, and know what you are willing to do to get what you want, decisions such as where to live are much easier to make.

Having said all that, we're now ready to go through the whole process from start to finish. Get out your pen and let's go!

Establish the big picture you want to create in the different areas of your life. Figure out what you want, your vision: That's the umbrella under which everything else you do will fall.

Achievement Areas

We all have different areas in our lives in which we would like to achieve different things. I am writing to the group that is near and dear to my heart: actors. We have a desire to excel in our craft. Part of what I am about to explain to you and have you apply is a concept that comes from Stephen Covey's book *The 7 Habits of Highly Effective People*.

One of the first things you want to do is identify the different areas of your life in which you would like to achieve some sort of result, whether big or small. Be specific. For example, for me a few of my areas are father, corporate trainer, actor, speaker, writer, friend to Butch, TV hosting, and so on.

What Are Your Achievement Areas?

Achievement Areas
1)
2)
3)
4)
5)
6)

Now, for the next part of the process, there is space for you in the form provided below to develop up to six of those areas in which it is important to achieve results as soon as possible.

Let me first explain the terms you will see in the forms below:

Vision: What do you want to achieve? How do you visualize success?

- o   "I want to have my own television program."
- o   "I want to have a host of important and useful industry contacts."
- o   "I want to be auditioning regularly (several each week)."
- o   "I want to make $XX each month."

Motivation: Why do you want what you want? Why is it important to you?

- o   "Because I want to be known by the right people so that they keep me in mind for auditions."
- o   "So that when they (my contacts: casting directors, directors, producers, etc.) have specific casting needs, they will think of me."
- o   "Because I will be earning a living only from my income as an artist."
- o   "Because I will finally have achieved my dream."

Activities: What things will you be doing on a daily basis that are necessary to achieve what you want? For example, in line with the example of the "vision" above:

- I might be making videos, have a Web site that provides resources for artists, doing regular postcard mailings, using trade papers and the internet and drop-offs to submit myself for projects, preparing my audition material and keeping it fresh, putting together several episodes of my program to pitch to producers, inventing new parts for my program, write my own play.

Three primary objectives: What three things absolutely must happen (big or small) for you to achieve your vision?

The following is an example of how you might want to think about your own achievement areas. This example contains some of my own personal thoughts almost four years ago. I have accomplished those goals and/or modified them and evolved.

EXAMPLE

Achievement Area 1:	Professional
What exactly do You Want to Achieve? :	I want to found my training and consulting company, that helps companies manage more effectively their human resources, plan strategically, manage time, improve selling skills and that helps individuals from all walks of life improve the quality of their lives by giving them the instruments (mental know-how) to help them change their lives for the positive.

Vision (briefly how you see it unfolding):	Motivation (the why?)
I will first find a training and consulting company that is well established, has a good reputation and that has a philosophy similar to my own. I will freelance with them while at the same time building up my own customer base. In the first year I will work mostly for them and gradually I will replace the days I work on that company's behalf with days I work with my own customers.	1. This kind of work will give me greater flexibility to manage my own schedule. 2. I will be able to determine how much money I want to make. 3. I will be able to spend more time with my son. 4. It will permit me the flexibility to study acting/hosting on my terms. 5. If I book a job as an actor or host, I can easily put the training business on hold.

I will offer consulting services over a period of time to my customers and I will offer both inter-company seminars as well as seminars for groups of individuals. The subjects will be business topics, strategic planning, time management, effective communication, sales and public speaking. In addition, I will offer seminars for individuals who are interested in changing their lives, but who are not sure how to do it.	6. I'll be able to work much more from home, which is what I like. 7. I will be able to set my own schedule. 8. I will be able to help companies improve their performance. 9. I'll be able to help people improve the quality of their lives.

What will you be doing or what kinds of activities will you be engaged in (specific actions) once you have reached your goal?

Using the internet in various ways to find customers, creating brochures, preparing proposals for my clients, selling, contacting people who sign up for my newsletters, writing newsletters, conducting seminars, training trainers who will work on my behalf, writing articles and books, maintaining the relationship with the company I'm freelancing with, creating new seminars, getting testimonials from the people who have experienced my seminars and putting them on the website, taking classes and courses myself to stay current on happenings in my field, building partnerships with other professionals who have complimentary products and investigate the possibility of doing joint ventures, staying in contact with my customers to ensure I keep giving them what they need, etc.

What are your 3 primary objectives or actions that will help you to achieve your vision in this achievement area?

1) Find out what my potential customers need. In other words, see what kind of training and consulting is most in demand.
2) Figure out what I will need to do to get started and how much startup capital I will need.
3) Find someone who has already done what I am setting out to do. Pick their brain to learn as much as possible about the mission on which I am about to embark.

Now it's your turn. Take some time and think about which six achievement areas you would like to work on and that, if you did, could give you the biggest boost in productivity and quality of life. Think about the results you could obtain both in the short term as well as in the long term (your vision of the future). If you are thinking professionally and more specifically about your acting career, try and define a specific goal that you would like to achieve and plan around that. Remember to be specific. If you are not specific enough, you risk not getting great results.

Achievement Area 1: _____

What exactly do You Want to Achieve? : _____

Vision (briefly how you see it unfolding):	Motivation (the why?)

What will you be doing or what kinds of activities will you be engaged in (specific actions) once you have reached your goal?

_____

_____

_____

What are your 3 primary objectives or actions that will help you to achieve your vision in this achievement area?

1)
2)
3)

Achievement Area 2: _____

**What exactly do You
Want to Achieve? :** _____

Vision (briefly how you see it unfolding):	Motivation (the why?)

**What will you be doing or what kinds of activities will you be
engaged in (specific actions) once you have reached your goal?**

_____

_____

_____

_____

**What are your 3 primary objectives or actions that
will help you to achieve your vision in this achievement area?**

1)
2)
3)

Achievement Area 3: _____

**What exactly do You
Want to Achieve? :** _____

Vision (briefly how you see it unfolding):	Motivation (the why?)

**What will you be doing or what kinds of activities will you be
engaged in (specific actions) once you have reached your goal?**

_____

_____

_____

_____

**What are your 3 primary objectives or actions that
will help you to achieve your vision in this achievement area?**

1)
2)
3)

Achievement Area 4: _____

What exactly do You
Want to Achieve? : _____

Vision (briefly how you see it unfolding):	Motivation (the why?)

What will you be doing or what kinds of activities will you be engaged in (specific actions) once you have reached your goal?

_____

_____

_____

_____

What are your 3 primary objectives or actions that will help you to achieve your vision in this achievement area?

1)

2)

3)

Achievement Area 5: _____

**What exactly do You
Want to Achieve? :** _____

Vision (briefly how you see it unfolding):	Motivation (the why?)

**What will you be doing or what kinds of activities will you be
engaged in (specific actions) once you have reached your goal?**

_____

_____

_____

_____

**What are your 3 primary objectives or actions that
will help you to achieve your vision in this achievement area?**

1)
2)
3)

Achievement Area 6: _____

What exactly do You
Want to Achieve? : _____

Vision (briefly how you see it unfolding):	Motivation (the why?)

What will you be doing or what kinds of activities will you be
engaged in (specific actions) once you have reached your goal?

_____

_____

_____

_____

What are your 3 primary objectives or actions that
will help you to achieve your vision in this achievement area?

1)
2)
3)

After you do this exercise in all the different areas of your life in which you would like to achieve results over the next twelve months, list below your top 10 objectives overall. These ten objectives are taken from the three at the bottom of each achievement area form. For example, in my case I might have a goal in the area of becoming an actor that might be getting new headshots and another goal in the area of being a father, which might be keeping my promise to my son and taking him to a football game. If you did the exercise and completed the forms for all six achievement areas then you will have a total of eighteen objectives. You now need to decide which ten are the most important and decide when you will have them accomplished. In other words, it's time to prioritize.

Once you set your goals, remember that creating and building your motivation is an important and continuous process to stay focused on. For this reason, make sure you answer the questions below after listing your top 10 objectives. Questions don't forget, are a great way to direct your focus, in this case to the positive. Put a specific date on your goals! Not approximate. Not "at the end of the month", but rather "by March 15th at noon." Put a specific date and time on your goal. If you do that, you'll be more likely to get it done.

Top 10 Goals

1)	By when?: _____
2)	By when?: _____
3)	By when?: _____
4)	By when?: _____
5)	By when?: _____
6)	By when?: _____
7)	By when?: _____
8)	By when?: _____
9)	By when?: _____
10)	By when?: _____

What will I gain by reaching these goals? What benefits will I have from reaching my goal?

_____

_____

What will change in me once I reach my goals? What kind of person will I have become?

_____

_____

**How will it make me feel having reached my objectives?

_____

_____

For this last question, list at least five emotions that you will feel. Saying that it will make you happy, for example, isn't enough. Force yourself to come up with five or more emotions. In doing this, you are training yourself to stretch your mind to find more possibilities in all situations you will encounter and most importantly, you are, in a subtle way, adding to the motivational power of you achieving your vision.

Also figure out what things must happen in order for you to achieve those top ten objectives. These are what I call "key factors for success," and they will help you in the next part of this exercise. They are key because if they don't happen, you won't achieve your vision. For example, for me to take my son to Africa on vacation, I will need $6,000 for the trip. If I don't have or somehow get hold of that money, that trip won't happen. So getting that money is a key factor for my success. Another objective could be signing up for on-going acting training. To do that, I will need a certain amount of money. Without that money, there will be no class.

So now, add another column to your list of objectives: Key Factors for Success and identify what they are.

Top 10 Goals	Date	Key Factors for Success
1)	By when? _____	1) 2) 3)
2)	By when?: _____	1) 2) 3)
3)	By when?: _____	1) 2) 3)
4)	By when?: _____	1) 2) 3)
5)	By when?: _____	1) 2) 3)
6)	By when?: _____	1) 2) 3)
7)	By when?: _____	1) 2) 3)
8)	By when?: _____	1) 2) 3)
9)	By when?: _____	1) 2) 3)
10)	By when?: _____	1) 2) 3)

Review your key factors for success and decide which, if any, you are willing to do. You might decide that you don't want to or are not willing to do them. If you are willing to take those actions, then they will become your main goals, your objectives. They must be clear and specific! Clarity up front will save you time, effort, and money down the road.

Note that deciding what you are willing to do is different than what you think you can do. Be positive. Think first about what it is you want to do, then think about how you will accomplish it. Don't limit your thinking in this phase. You must objectively state what needs to happen, however simple or extremely difficult you think it might be. This is not the phase in which you try and figure out the feasibility or whether something is doable or not. You are thinking objectively about what needs to happen.

Prioritize your goals so that you can tackle them systematically. If you're not good yet at managing multiple tasks, trying to do all of them at once can set you back and demotivate you; doing this could also take you longer to achieve what you want or, worse yet, some things you might not achieve at all. We'll talk later on in the business section about multitasking, a skill that if mastered, can project you forward much more quickly.

Remember that to reach one big objective, you will rarely do it all at once. Each of those key factors for success we talked about (the things that must happen in order for you to reach an objective) is really a little objective that will help us meet the bigger one. In other words, each key factor is just one of the things you must do to reach your objective. As you achieve them one by one, you will be motivated and will be able to see that you are slowly reaching your bigger goal. But you have to stay the course.

Thinking about the person you are today, are you the person who will enjoy the success you are dreaming of? In other words, do you have what it takes in this moment to achieve what you want? Do you have the necessary skills? Do you have the technical knowledge, the steadfastness, the discipline, the drive, the determination, or whatever it takes to reach your objectives? It's possible you have the skills or you, like most of us, believe that there is something you need to improve on. We can always improve on something, right? We never stop learning. Be honest with yourself here. For example, maybe you want to become a successful playwright but are not yet ready. Maybe you don't have the writing skills or the necessary experience to achieve that kind of success yet; therefore, you must begin acquiring the necessary skills.

If you want to become an actor or be a good enough one to land a principal role on a prime-time series or on a soap, you might just have to apply yourself and dedicate yourself to studying and taking the right classes to improve your skills. It could also be that you need more memory work, voice enhancement, diction, movement, accent correction, or whatever.

So the question becomes, "What kind of person do you need to become to achieve the success you desire?" In order to be successful at what you are striving for, you must act as if you are already doing it. What qualities or characteristics will you have that you haven't yet fully developed? Someone who is barely making ends meet and who has the desire to become rich and who has made that his goal can't achieve that goal thinking and behaving like a poor person. He must think and reason and act like a rich person and begin to either do or learn how to do the things that rich people do; otherwise, it is doubtful that he will ever make it. To do that, he needs a new skill set.

What kinds of things, then, will you do each and every day to make sure you reach your goal? Be specific as to which actions you will be engaged in.

_____

_____

_____

_____

_____

_____

> *"Reaching your objectives in themselves will not be enough to make you happy in the long run. It is the person you will become along the way, that will ultimately give you a profound sense of lasting achievement."*
>
> *Anthony Robbins*

Resource check: Do you think you are doing everything possible to achieve the success you want? Take stock of the resources you already have at your disposal as well as those you must acquire: It is great to think you already possess inside you all the resources you need. All you have to do is bring them out. This might not sound easy, but it is possible. This means that if you don't know something that you will need to accomplish your goal, you must know how to find out, who to ask to make sure it gets done. If you want to be successful, you must not accept anything less from yourself.

Easier said than done, but no matter what your life has been like to date, where you come from, how much or how little success you have enjoyed, I bet you have some hidden ability that you can bring to fruition, some ability that can help you achieve even better results than you are currently getting. What makes me say that? It is a known fact that we human beings rarely live up to our full potential!

The next step in the process is the monthly plan. Now you are beginning to focus and narrow down which activities you will accomplish this month. You can't do everything, so you must prioritize. That's what this portion of the process is all about. Focus.

Monthly Planning

Prioritizing Your Goals

What actions would you like to be able to do this month that would help you get closer to your goals? Put all your ideas on the table:	
_____	_____
_____	_____
_____	_____
_____	_____
_____	_____

Since you might not be able to do them all, focus on just some of those ideas:	
_____	_____
_____	_____
_____	_____
_____	_____
_____	_____

Of those ideas, which 6 are the most important that you need to do this month? Prioritize.	
1)	4)
2)	5)
3)	6)

Narrowing It Down Further

In the form below entitled, "Main Objectives For The Month of
_____", the person you put in the "Responsible" column must be some-
one who is fully accountable and responsible for accomplishing that action and

not just someone who you need to ask or someone who "said" he would help you. If anyone else is responsible for completing the action, make sure they can be held responsible. If not, it may not get done. In most cases, *you* should be the responsible person! You don't ever want to tell yourself or others that it was somebody else's fault you didn't accomplish what you wanted. Remember that it is your plan and ultimately you are responsible for what gets done and what doesn't.

Also, going through all this work could be fruitless if you don't put a specific date on each of your objectives.

Main Objectives For The Month of _____		

Objective 1: _____	To be completed by:_____	
Action	Responsible	Date

Objective 2: _____	To be completed by:_____	
Action	Responsible	Date

Objective 3: _____	To be completed by:_____	
Action	Responsible	Date
_____	_____	_____
_____	_____	_____
_____	_____	_____
_____	_____	_____
_____	_____	_____
_____	_____	_____
_____	_____	_____
_____	_____	_____

Objective 4: _____	To be completed by:_____	
Action	Responsible	Date
_____	_____	_____
_____	_____	_____
_____	_____	_____
_____	_____	_____
_____	_____	_____
_____	_____	_____
_____	_____	_____
_____	_____	_____

Objective 5: _____	To be completed by:_____	
Action	Responsible	Date
_____	_____	_____
_____	_____	_____
_____	_____	_____
_____	_____	_____
_____	_____	_____
_____	_____	_____
_____	_____	_____
_____	_____	_____

Objective 6: _____	To be completed by:_____	
Action	Responsible	Date
_____	_____	_____
_____	_____	_____
_____	_____	_____
_____	_____	_____
_____	_____	_____
_____	_____	_____
_____	_____	_____
_____	_____	_____

Figure out each step you will need to take, each action necessary to reach each objective. I can't emphasize that enough. Be specific! Before going to an away game, Coach Carpenter would have us get dressed mentally after we had already packed our equipment. He would have us close our eyes and imagine walking into the locker room at our opponents' field house and unpacking our bags; then he would tell us to imagine getting dressed: putting on our shoes, socks, pads in our pants, shoulder pads, shirt, pants, mouthpieces, and so on. He did this so we wouldn't forget anything. I suggest you do the same when imagining the result you want and all the things that absolutely must happen, step by step.

Take each one of your big goals (your top 10), your key factors for success (the things that must happen), and break them down into smaller chunks. Remember that big goals consist of a series of little ones. For example, one of your key factors for success might be to select a school where you can study your craft. The smaller goals that will help you achieve that bigger one might be to research different acting methods, find schools that teach those methods, go and interview the teachers, set your budget, determine how much time you have to study, and on which days. Each one of those areas can be a key factor for success for that particular goal. Around each one, you will have a plan on how to complete it. You can think of it like a tree: Without the twigs and little branches, the tree wouldn't be what it is.

Put together a series of action items for this objective: Focus on one key factor of success at a time. Be specific in all the action items you need in order to achieve that little objective. Imagine and visualize what success will look like when you have finished. If you can visualize it, then you will be more likely to do it. If you can't visualize what it is you want in the end, then how do you think you will be able to achieve your goal? And don't forget the power of questions in figuring this out. For example, for your objective to get head shots taken, you might ask yourself some questions like the following:

1. What are they for—TV, commercials, print, film, theater?

2. Do they need to be black and white or color?

3. What strong points do I want to bring out in the pictures? What weaknesses do I not want to emphasize?

4. How much do I want to spend? Why is that my budget? How much is necessary to spend to get good-quality shots?

5. Where can I find information about photographers?

6. Which photographers are good at shooting my type?

7. Who can I trust to give me a good recommendation for a good photographer?

8. Do I need just one or two types of shots, or do I need different looks or types of shots?

9. What else can/will I do with these pictures besides send them to casting directors and agents?

10. Will I be using some of them for postcards or other types of self-marketing material?

11. Do I need certain types of shots for a photo book or to create a photo gallery on my Web site?

12. How do I need to work with the photographer to get the best results?

13. What can I expect from my photographer?

14. What are the pitfalls to avoid?

These are just a few questions you might want to ask yourself. At any rate, you should think of the right questions to ask yourself that fit your goals. Answering them will give you greater clarity of action.

Put specific dates next to each action item: If you don't put it on the calendar, you won't get it done unless you are super motivated and are eating, sleeping, and drinking this goal. Get in the habit of writing down everything around your goals. It will be helpful in the future when you go to analyze your results. You will see and figure out what worked and what didn't and why. You'll see if your planning was too lax and realize that maybe you could have done more versus what you had planned to accomplish. By the same token, you will see if your planning was too aggressive and where you tried to do too much.

Pushing dates back is too easy. Don't do it unless absolutely necessary. And be honest with yourself. If you don't do something you know you should have, it can mean different things, but most often it simply means that you haven't made it important enough to yourself, that you are trying to do too many things at the same time or that your deadline wasn't realistic in the first place. So, as you make your goals and set your objectives, create the necessary motivation around each one. I've said it before and I'll say it again: find as many reasons as possible why you *need* to get this done.

Monitor your progress daily: Get in the habit of keeping tabs on how you are doing versus your goal. For example, if you said you would find a photographer by March 30 and it is now April 15 and you still haven't found one, that's not good, because you should have known that before. Monitoring your results daily will keep you on track *before* the deadline hits so that you can react and keep things on schedule.

People who are serious about losing weight are on the scales constantly, making sure their diets and exercise routines are working. If you are serious about your goals, you will check your progress however often you feel is necessary to keep you focused.

Analyze your results: Get in the habit of continuously asking yourself what is working and what is not, what you could have done better and what you are doing well that you should keep on doing or reinforce. Just because you tried something once or twice and didn't get the expected results doesn't mean you shouldn't do it. Remember what Picasso and Thomas Edison did? Figure out why it didn't work, make the necessary adjustments, and go for it again. Later you will see that I was auditioning for a while without getting any callbacks. I had to stop and take stock of what I was doing, evaluate it, make changes. I then started getting better results. I keep harping on this because it is often seen as not necessary or important. Instead it is crucial to the success of your projects.

Planning and Scheduling

Once you identify your major goals and objectives to accomplish for the month, make sure you get them done. When planning your time, there are some basic rules you will want to follow.

Look at the diagram below. It demonstrates that in order to ensure you get the important things done, those major actions you want to accomplish, you must fill your schedule first and foremost with those big chunks, the really important and sometimes even more difficult things that need to be done. Don't put in the little meaningless time-wasters first. Here are three rules to follow when planning:

1. Put the big things you want to accomplish into your calendar first. These are the things you want to make sure you do even if you don't get anything else done. They are that important! Train yourself to calculate how much time you will need to accomplish each task.

2. Leave some space in your agenda. If you fill up every minute in your schedule, you risk being disappointed. Why? Because some unforeseen things will inevitably come up. Leave space for them. They will happen!

3. Put in last the little things that won't make a big difference if you don't get them done.

Effective Planning

The following diagram shows how you must plan to ensure you get everything done. Put the bigger, most important things in your schedule first and then add everything else.

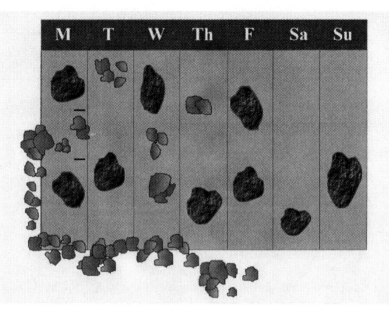

Now, with what you have just learned, how will you plan your week to get yourself on the road to achieving your goals and make sure you get done what you plan? Go ahead and fill out this schedule for your activities next week.

Monday	Tuesday	Wednesday	Thursday	Friday
8 -------------	8 -------------	8 -------------	8 ------------	8 -------------
9 ----------------	9 ----------------	9 ---------------	9 ---------------	9 -----------------
10 -------------	10 -------------	10 --------------	10 -------------	10 --------------
11 --------------	11 --------------	11 --------------	11 ---------------	11 --------------
12 --------------	12 --------------	12 --------------	12 ---------------	12 --------------
1 ----------------	1 ----------------	1 ----------------	1 ----------------	1 ----------------
2 ----------------	2 ----------------	2 ----------------	2 ----------------	2 ----------------
3 ----------------	3 ----------------	3 ----------------	3 ----------------	3 ----------------
4 ---------------	4 ----------------	4 ----------------	4 ----------------	4 ----------------
5 ---------------	5 ----------------	5 ---------------	5 ----------------	5 ----------------
6 ---------------	6 ----------------	6 ---------------	6 ---------------	6 ----------------
7 ---------------	7 ----------------	7 --------------	7 --------------	7 ---------------

Daily Planning

Daily Check

At the beginning of each day, review your goals and objectives to see if any changes are required. Your plan must be living. That means you must check it often to ensure that you stay on track.

Think about this: If you have ever flown anywhere, you may or may not know that a plane must adjust its course frequently. If it never adjusts its course, it will not reach its destination because of winds that can knock it off course. You must continuously pilot your plane and keep it on course.

Your guiding questions will also help you. Instead of asking yourself what you *have to do* today, ask yourself, "What are my objectives today?" "What are the results that I want to achieve by the end of the day?"

Remember, you don't *have to* do anything but pay your taxes and die!

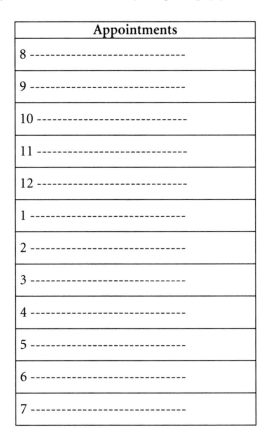

Appointments
8 -----------------------------
9 -----------------------------
10 -----------------------------
11 -----------------------------
12 -----------------------------
1 -----------------------------
2 -----------------------------
3 -----------------------------
4 -----------------------------
5 -----------------------------
6 -----------------------------
7 -----------------------------

Congratulations on Putting Together Your Initial Plan!

Any plan is only as good as the person who executes it. Your plan is meant to be living. Don't just put it in the drawer and forget about it. Keep it visible at all times. Things will change and you will have to modify what you wrote. Remember, you must keep your plane on course.

Lastly in this section, I want to tell you that reading this book won't necessarily grant you 100 percent success. In fact, that would be a very unrealistic expectation. However, if you follow what I've outlined here and go through the exercises, this book can significantly increase your chances of achieving what you want.

CHAPTER 11

Focus

How to Improve Your Focus Tenfold: Effective Time Management

Have you ever tried to accomplish something important and different things kept coming up to impede your progress? Did you ever stop to think about why that is? One of the things that keep us from focusing all our attention on our goals is distraction.

Gearing Your Time Management toward Results

By now you've probably gotten the message that *The 7 Habits of Highly Effective People* is a book you should read. I have no gain whether you read the book or not. There is a reason why it topped the best-seller list for at least a couple years. Anyway, Stephen Covey talks about the four quadrants and where we spend our time. He talks about measuring time in terms of both urgency and importance.

As you can see in the following diagram, he talks about things that are

1. urgent and important;

2. urgent but not important;

3. not urgent but important;

4. not urgent and not important.

It is important to note that these things are attached to the things we do, not necessarily because of what they represent, but because of the meaning we give them. In other words, not always, but very often, you decide what's important and what is urgent. For example, if you are in a conversation with a person and your cell phone rings, some people will answer the phone immediately no matter what and no matter who it is, because they consider it a must. Others will wait until after their conversation, then call back whoever called them. In another example, maybe a friend falls sick and faints. Some would immediately take the sick friend to the hospital. Others would simply put him down to rest and look after him until he feels better. For the first person, it was something that needed immediate medical attention. For the second person, the level of importance attached to the event was dialed down a notch. It was obviously important, but not enough to warrant immediate attention from a doctor.

So what are the *urgent and important* things we deal with every day, the things in quadrant one? Telephone calls. A customer might call you and request to see you immediately or in the same day. A friend calls with urgency in her voice and needs to talk to you right away. On the other hand, there could be things that really require your immediate attention: A family member or someone close to you needs immediate medical attention, someone needs to be helped physically right away or it could be detrimental to their health. In all these examples, the question is, "Is it really necessary to act in that specific moment and if so, is important that you turn your entire day upside down to address this issue? Could it be done in another way?"

Urgent but not important: There are things that may be important to someone else and that you need to deal with right away. For instance, your boss might ask you to develop a project and have it on his desk by the morning. You would then need to shift focus and get that done. A friend might seem desperate and ask for your immediate help. You respond right away and oblige. Both those things are important but not necessarily for you. They are important to the person who asked you, but you have other priorities.

Not urgent but very important: This is where planning and preparation comes in for whatever you want to do. It is extremely important to have clarity on where you're going and on how you will get there, but it needn't be rushed. Planning at its best is done when there is time to think things through properly. Time you set aside just for that. Successful people, people who habitually achieve great results in just about anything, plan their moves in advance. Now go back to your monthly objectives and look to see if you've planned this time into your schedule.

Not urgent and not important: This is where we waste a lot of our time doing things that are neither urgent nor important. For example, spending too much time during a break at work. Breaks are important and essential to keep you focused and productive, but a fifteen-minute coffee break that turns into thirty minutes because you're socializing with a colleague might be too much if you are on a tight schedule. It could also be as simple as not having a plan for what you want to achieve, so you are easily distracted. For example, you turn to the Internet to look up some important information on a casting Web site and end up wasting a half hour on something else that catches your eye instead of accomplishing what you set out to do. Neither is important or urgent.

Where Do You Spend Most Of Your Time?

Someone once said that the degree of success one enjoys is directly proportionate to how one spends his time. If this is true, how successful should you be? Answer the questions below.

Urgent and Important: Pressure

What urgent and important things do you do? Over the last week, what percentage of your time did you spend in this area?

_____

_____

_____

Urgent but Not Important: Dissatisfaction

What things do you do that are or seem to be urgent, even when you know there are other more important things to accomplish? How much time do you spend doing them? What percentage of your time did you spend doing things in this area?

_____

_____

_____

Not Urgent but Important: Being Proactive

What non-urgent things do you do because they are important? How much time do you spend doing them? What percentage of your time did you spend in this area?

_____

_____

_____

Not Urgent and Not Important: Distractions

When you are feeling stressed, how do you distract yourself? How do you take your mind off things and relax? How much time do you usually spend doing it? Over the last week, what percentage of your time did you spend in this area?

_____

_____

_____

It is logical that the more time you spend doing things that are not urgent, but very important (planning and doing things in advance of when they need to be done), the better results you can expect to achieve. Where do you spend most of your time, and what effect is it having on the results you get?

How to Reach Your Goals Faster by Pruning Yourself

In the springtime, trees and bushes must be pruned so they can bloom fully and freely. Applying this practice to us people, sometimes we need to prune ourselves of the people who keep us from blooming.

One of the rules to success in any field is to surround yourself with winners and not losers. It's better to surround yourself with people who can stimulate your growth, people from whom you can learn things that will help you on your journey in life. We already talked about people who are successful in everything they do. We also talked about what those people have in common. By now I'm sure you have someone in mind who you consider to be an achiever. Right? Good.

I have someone in mind too. This person is a real go-getter. He doesn't take no for an answer. He knows what he wants, and he persists until he gets it. Sometimes, unfortunately, he steps on people to get where he is going. While I personally don't condone the "by any means necessary" rule, I do admire this person greatly for his drive, determination, and his strong will to achieve and win.

One thing in particular that I noticed while studying this person, whom I will call Bill, is the company he keeps. I never see him hanging around anyone who isn't on the same mission, who doesn't share his interests, and, most importantly, with whom he can't learn or share experiences at an equal level. The people he hangs around are all go-getters, just like he is. They are all driven, just like he is. They are positive thinkers, just like he is. They create opportunities, just like he does. And they are all achievers, just like he is.

Studying this person made me look closer at my own life—my goals and the people I hung around with. I would like you to do the same; think about who your real "friends" are. Forget about the fact that we are sometimes judged by the company we keep. Let's just think about reaching goals and how we spend our time reaching those goals.

The Dead Branches

If we are going to reach our goals, like Bill, we must be focused all the time! I began to look at the people I was wasting my time with. People who were negative. People who were always complaining. People who, when you tell them about your goals and how you want to achieve them, they just look at you with admiration as if to say, "Boy, Tony, you're always on a mission!" Or "Well, if you say so, but I think it will be difficult to do." Sometimes they offer you fake encouragement, and some even hope that you will fail so you can stay around and keep them company.

These are the same people who you call to stay in touch, but who never or rarely call you. You run up your phone bill talking to them, even though they don't care as much about you as you think you do about them. These are the people with whom you visit only at their house; they can never come to you because they're too busy or because it's never the right time. These people couldn't care less about you! In fact, they are rarely there when you really need them. They are selfish and self-centered.

These are the people who often complain but never do anything to change the situation. These are the same folks who, when they talk about their personal circumstances, they complain for as long as you let them, but when you ask them how they will make things better, they respond, "I don't know." These are the people who have the nerve to criticize you for your efforts in trying to achieve your lofty goals, even when they haven't done anything to reach their own. Or worse yet, they don't even have any goals to reach.

Some years ago, I began to cut the dead branches from my tree, canceling numbers from my telephone memory and vowing never to call again unless they made some positive steps toward me. It was difficult in some cases, because they're not all bad people; they just aren't the people I want accompanying me on my journey, because they are more of a burden than a benefit. They were robbing me of valuable time. Just think about it. The five minutes here and the half hour there begin to add up. It's time I could have been spending on something for me, or working or doing something for myself.

The Buds

Prune your tree and cut away these dead branches before your tree dies. Don't let that happen! Get away from them and find people who have the same ambitions as you. The same drive and determination. The same will to succeed. The same positive mental attitude. These are the people you can bounce ideas off of, because, even if you don't have the same goals in common, they can give you valuable insight and advice that can help you be successful. They can be a source of inspiration, because they are going through what you are going through or maybe they have already done it. These are the people who have experience in reaching goals and in going after their dreams. These are the folks who can share their positive experiences and their mistakes on their way to success, things that will inevitably help you reach your destination.

I want you to be successful. Even if you keep the kind of negative company we talked about, that doesn't mean you can't be successful, but it will probably take you a lot longer to get where you are going.

Get rid of the losers and you will be more productive and will have more energy and time to do the things necessary to reach your goals! You will be more focused.

KEY FACTOR #4

Basic Business Skills:
You the Actor. You the Company.
You the Business.

*Good business sense at the start,
pays big dollars down the road.*

CHAPTER 12

21 Principles of Business

After fifteen years of living corporate business, I believe that the principles that apply in business also apply to promoting oneself as an artist. Let me explain.

There are certain steps an entrepreneur must take if he is to ensure success in his new business. These are the same steps that an existing and well-established business must take to stay abreast of things and to ensure that things continue to run smoothly. However, both entertainers and many, many companies consider these steps to be a waste of time and therefore ignore them.

Oftentimes, owners of some companies think they can manage things from their gut. It is the law of business that at some point you will probably suffer a downturn in revenues. The trick is to stay ahead of the game, continuing to train even when things are going well, continuing to invest in growing the business even when you don't think it's necessary. Research and development of new products and in new ways to grow and promote the business are also concepts that applies to any field, even that of being an artist.

To keep informed about industry trends, aside from the trade papers like Backstage, Show Business, Theatrical Index, Hollywood Reporter you will want to research some of the Web sites I mentioned earlier. At any rate the resources are many. I found the following some excerpts on the SAG website for example, that talked about how union roles on television have suffered due to the increase in reality programming. In particular, episodic television was mentioned to have taken the hardest hit. Although I had hoped to find more recent information there, it still gave me an overall idea of how things are. On the U. S. Department of Labor, Bureau of Statistics web page, I found some interesting information about the overall job outlook for actors. They also went on to talk in detail about actor earnings.

JOB OUTLOOK   "Employment of actors, producers, and directors is expected to grow about as fast as the average for all occupations through 2014. Although a growing number of people will aspire to enter these professions, many will leave the field early because the work—when it is available—is hard, the hours are long, and the pay is low. Competition for jobs will be stiff, in part because of the large number of highly trained and talented actors auditioning for roles generally exceeds the number of parts that become available. Only performers with the most stamina and talent will find regular employment."

Unfortunately the information on those two sites was a bit outdated, but I know for a fact that the earnings numbers and the overall situation haven't changed so terribly much. My fellow actors, we are up against great odds.

If we want to excel in our chosen field as actors, as the free-lance professionals that actors are, as the business people we have to be, then we must be proactive. More importantly, we must *know what to do* to be proactive in promoting ourselves—the artists, the companies, and the businesses.

21 Business Principles

Here are twenty-one things we can learn from the corporate world that can help us further our careers.

1. Study the Market

Get as much market information as you can. Find out "the lay of the land," how the industry works and who your competition is. Businesses and companies know the environment in which they operate. They know where they fit in, how big the industry is, what their market share is. They know who the big players are, who their competition is, and what they have to offer in terms of products, services, and prices. They know how they operate and what they provide to their customers. They keep abreast of industry developments and things that can change the effect that their efforts can have for the good!

Take Away

   a.   Know where you can get information about market demographics, breakdown by race, types of roles, trends in the industry, and so on.

   b.   Know the right people—directors, producers, casting directors who cater specifically for your type, agents, schools, teachers, and so on.

   c.   Know where you can get the resources you need for résumés, head shots, technique classes, voice, diction, movement, classics, show reels, demo CDs, informational suggestions, and so on.

   d.   Industry and trade papers. There are more than just one or two. Find out which ones are available and which ones give you the best and most complete information.

   e.   Know your genre. A casting director once told me that if you want to be on television, you need to watch television. If you want to be on soaps, prime-time, daytime, hosted programs, and so on, you need to watch them.

Here are some places to start gathering good information. There are certainly others, but these are the ones that I frequently referred to:

The Unions:

SAG (Screen Actors Guild): www.sag.org
AFTRA (American Federation of Television and Radio Artists): www.aftra.com
Actors' Equity: www.actorsequity.com

Statistics:

U.S. Department of Labor, Bureau of Labor Statistics:
www.bls.gov/oco/ocos093.htm

General Information:

Backstage: www.backstage.com
Ross Reports: www.rossreports.com
Show Business: www.showbusiness.com
The Hollywood Reporter: www.hollywoodreporter.com
Time Out: www.timeout.com
New York/LA Agencies Publication: gives information about agents and what exactly they are looking for.
All the above-mentioned websites also have printed publications as well.

General Info and Coaching:

Brian O'Neil: www.actingasabusiness.com
Leslie Becker: www.organizedactor.com
Janice Hoffmann: www.successissweetest.com
Sue Porter Henderson: www.hendersonenterprises.com

2. Unique Selling Proposition

When businesses put together a selling strategy around one of their products, one question they ask themselves is, "What's our unique selling proposition (USP)?" In other words, what is unique about our product that could appeal to consumers? Even in a market that is saturated with similar types of products, businesses need to find their USP, because it is what sets them apart from the rest.

To do this, you must know yourself very well; know who you *really* are and what you have to offer. Here are some questions and things you might want to consider if you haven't already:

What is your product? Your product is you! That's your baby. You need to know how to market it, how to create and market your brand, how to protect it. If you don't, you'd better find out; otherwise, you will be just like the thousands of others out there trying to get noticed. Remember the question "How many different ways are there…?" Think outside of the box.

What about you? What is your type? Do you know? Who are the producers, directors, casting directors, agents who cater to your type? Could you be interesting for them? If so, why?

Evaluate yourself: your strengths (your strong points as an individual), weaknesses (things you need to improve on), opportunities (things that now would be a great time to start or try and accomplish) and threats (things that if you don't fix or do something about them immediately, they will prohibit you from continuing on your path to success). This is all about taking stock of your present situation, of your starting point, of the resources and of the situation that you find yourself with at the beginning of your mission to achieve your goal. Don't get ahead of yourself. This is not an exercise in trying to find solutions to your weaknesses. That comes later. Simply list the things in all four of those areas. And that's it. It's a snapshot of the moment, which becomes a point of reference for the next steps of setting up the plan.

All the aforementioned things will help you to better understand what your USP is.

Here's an example of what my swot analysis looked like a few years ago as I was considering becoming an actor/host:

My Strengths	My Weaknesses (Areas to Develop)
• Maturity • Quick Learner • Business skills • Energy level to change careers at midlife (not to be underestimated!) • Communication/public speaking skills • Business résumé (NIKE, Levi's) • Financial resources • Creativity • Drive and determination	• Didn't really comprehend what being an actor, TV host really meant. • Knew very little about the industry • No acting training/low skill level • Based in Italy, far away from NY/LA, which is where I need/want to be located to be a U.S. actor • No industry contacts
Opportunities	Threats
• Train as an actor • Use my business/entrepreneurial skills to create a way to promote myself that is different from what other actors do, to get noticed • Move back to the U.S. (Yeah!!!!!) • Start my own business • Create my own TV program • Create my own content (write)	• Not planning a tight budget (the risk is without good budgeting, finding myself only halfway through my project and then have to go back to work in the traditional sense)! • Not taking the first step, which is to dedicate myself full-time to my goal. (I had to make a tough decision and leap out of the corporate world and commit 100 percent!)

When looking for the answers to those questions (strengths, weaknesses, opportunities, threats), remember the question we discussed earlier: "What kind of person do I need to become in order to do what I want?" You might need help to give yourself an objective evaluation. If so, then seek it out until you get what you feel is an honest evaluation of yourself. It takes courage to ask someone what they think of you. If you don't have that much courage, could be a sign that you need to rethink what it is you want. Seek out people who can give you objective feedback for your work as an actor. In the meantime, give it a shot. Put together your own swot analysis of yourself.

My Strengths	My Weaknesses (areas to develop)
Opportunities	Threats

This fits in with the concept of differentiation. I once took a seminar at the Learning Annex that was about how to become a seminar leader. The speaker said that we had to become an expert at something. One lady raised her hand and said that she has a subject that she is very knowledgeable about but someone was already offering seminars in that area.

The speaker responded, "So what!" No one will do it like you.

For my consulting and training business, my USP is that my seminars and presentations are very different, innovative, and entertaining, which makes them memorable. The name of my company is perfectly in line with that: JOLTEN Educational Events and Entertainment. "Jolt" is what I give my audiences when they see me speak, and "EN" stands for "entertainment."

Take Away

In a sea of artists wanting to do the same thing as you, and given the fact that your product is *you*, what is your USP? What is unique about you? What do you bring to the table when conducting your business or promoting yourself that is unique to you?

3. Your Customers

It is vital to know exactly whom you are marketing your products and services to. Many small businesses fail for this reason. They try and market to anyone and everyone, thinking that if they canvas the territory, they will have greater success. On the contrary. The more focused companies are in marketing to their target consumer, the more effective their efforts and the return will be on their advertising spending.

When I was working for Nike, I used to have customers who wanted to choose from our entire line of more than eight hundred models of shoes. We placed our shoes in the marketplace based on where consumers would go to find them. It didn't make sense to place a lot of top-of-the-line shoes in stores whose consumers had extremely limited budgets.

This also happens on the Internet. People set up businesses and try and market to "the world," thinking that their message will reach everyone. However, their marketing message or ad ends up being so generic that many people don't feel like it speaks to them, and sales are thus limited. On the other hand, there are those who market to a tight niche. The tighter the better. When ads are written for those consumers, the messages hit home, because they are tailored specifically for them.

Take Away

Who do you want to market yourself to? Saying you simply want to market to casting directors and agents is too vague. Which specific casting directors, teachers, schools, agents, producers, directors, and so on, and why them? Think about whether or not you could be interesting for them and why.

---

4. Vision

Successful companies know exactly where they want to take their companies. They put a lot of thought into this and communicate it to the entire organization. They think about all the things you read about before. More specifically, they think about where they would like to be five years from now, what role they want to play in the market, how big of a market share they want, who their customers will be, what products and services they will offer, and so forth.

Take Away

Have you ever asked yourself, "Where would you like to be in five years?" I'm asking you now. Where would you like to be? What would you like to be doing in five years? When you wake up in the morning five years from now, what exactly will you do? Where exactly will you go? Where will you be living? What kind of house? What kind of acting (or other) job will you have? How much money will you be earning? There are many more questions to answer. Be specific.

---

5. Mission

The company's mission is its philosophy. A mission statement simply says what the company is about or in what way it intends to achieve its vision while serving as a behavioral guide for everything the company does.

For example, JOLTEN Educational Events and Entertainment has the following mission statement:

JOLTEN facilitates the development of human potential with the purpose of aiding organizations, teams and individuals in the achievement of extraordinary results. JOLTEN will achieve this by delivering training with great impact and in innovative ways that will be memorable and inspire participants to take action.

This is the reason that the company has the name it has. JOLT (En)tertainment!

Everything JOLTEN does—every seminar, speech, coaching session, book, newsletter that my company puts out—must be in line with the mission statement. If it isn't, I'm not living true to my values, and I should probably change my mission.

My current mission in this stage of my acting and hosting career is:

Make the most money, in the least amount of time, with the least amount of effort possible, to allow me to have the greatest amount of flexibility possible so I can concentrate on my craft.

Along with this goes the identification of your values. For example, my own personal values are energy, honesty, courage, credibility, method, innovation, determination, professionalism, and results.

Take Away

What are your values? What's your philosophy? What's your mission? What are you all about? What is your guiding light?

_____

_____

_____

6. Objectives/Goals

Successful companies don't just wake up in the morning and decide what they will do that day. They have short-, medium-, and long-term goals. The goals are specific and clear. The bigger the organization, the more difficult it is to ensure that everyone knows what the company is setting out to achieve. For this reason the goals must be clear and easy to understand.

Good goals and objectives have the following characteristics:

- Set S.M.A.R.T. goals:
  o   S: Specific
  o   M: Measurable
  o   A: Achievable
  o   R: Relevant
  o   T: Timely

In business, there is an unspoken law among company directors and sales directors: When it comes time to set sales targets for your people, listen to what your salespeople have to say, but never give them the final word as to what they think is possible. Why? In all my years as a sales director, I remember just one selling season in which my salespeople told me that the target I gave them to reach was attainable. The rest of the time they told me they didn't think the target was reachable. They told me that I was crazy. They told me that my bosses were crazy. However, we usually reached or exceeded our targets or we came damned close. Listening to the salespeople could be dangerous and stunt your growth. You could end up with results that are below the company's potential. So how does that apply to being an artist? If you set your goals too low, you will likely get results that are not in line with your real potential. If you want to achieve greatness, you have to think like a great person and go for the gusto, as they used to say in the old Budweiser commercials!

Take Away

Are your objectives clear? Are they SMART? Are you shooting for the stars? If not, go back and clarify them now.

---

7. Planning

Once companies have clarity of vision, a mission, and clear objectives, they use that information to put together a very detailed plan, just like we did earlier. It is so specific that each individual in the organization knows what his/her exact role is, why they are doing it, and when they must do it. They know an action is on the plan because it will help ensure that the company vision will be reached. There is commitment to the plan's achievement at all levels of the organization. It must be clear, solid, and everyone is held accountable for the actions for which he/she is responsible.

They put together a strategic, long-term plan and then a yearly business plan to ensure they will stay on track over the five-year period. These plans are living, which means they are constantly reviewed, monitored, and modified if necessary to stay the course.

By now, I hope you've already started working on your plan. Keep it alive!

Take Away

How about your plan? Is it solid and clear, and do you hold yourself accountable for everything you have written? Is your plan specific or vague? Is it results-oriented? Is it your plan or someone else's? Is it all about what you want to do or what someone else wants you to do? Are you motivated to execute it?

---

8. The Organization: Roles and Responsibilities

At this point, once we know where we're going, it's time to figure out what kind of organizational structure will help us achieve our vision. Companies look at how the individual elements of sales, marketing, finance, human resources, information technology, shipping, and so on, fit into their plan. They have to decide which departments to set up and how many people each department will need and what each person will do on a daily basis.

That's where roles and responsibilities come in. One of the most important things for the smooth functioning of companies is that everyone knows what his or her specific roles and responsibilities are. Seems simple, but if every company's employees had clarity about what their roles and responsibilities are, then consultants and corporate trainers would have less work.

So what does this mean for an artist? If you want great results, it is unlikely that you can do everything alone. And while you don't need to hire employees, you will need a photographer, teachers, agents, industry contacts with producers, directors, playwrights, technicians, secretaries, casting directors, schools, institutions, associations, industry publications, and so on.

Make a list of all the services and types of people you need that will help you reach your goals. First concentrate on the types of services you need (i.e., photographer, teacher, etc.). After you do that and assign to each of these individuals your expectations, then you can go on to the next step of working on competencies.

So, for example: You know you need a teacher. Have you chosen a school based on certain criteria or have you chosen it just because you know someone else who is going there? Do you know what you are looking for? Have you shopped around? If you haven't, how do you know there isn't another method of acting that is more conducive to your learning style?

Let me share with you my criteria for the choice of an acting school (these are not in order):

- Teachers have experience acting
- Provides ongoing training (ongoing classes)
- Has a base technique
- Has a technique that is conducive to my style of learning
- Has a technique that gets me results as quickly as possible and that is easy to use
- Faculty that is serious and professional

- Teachers who care about my learning, who push me and challenge me, and who will kick me in the butt if necessary
- Teachers who don't treat me like a number
- Teachers who take pride in the development of their students and who really care
- Cost of classes within my budget
- Class times suitable for my schedule
- Offers a variety of classes that are complementary to each other so that I can stay at the same school and practice the technique in all the classes I take there. (It helps to stay focused instead of taking a technique class at one school, audition technique at another, scene study at another, and so on. However, it might not be possible to do everything at one school. This is what I preferred a few years ago, when I was just starting out. Most schools usually specialize in one thing or do one thing really well. If you can find a school that does more than one thing well, that's a plus. Just a thought.)
- Doesn't play favorites. Everyone is treated equally and fairly

These are *my* criteria. When you are choosing a school, I would suggest for you to have some criteria of your own. If you don't know what you are looking for and why, then any school and any teacher (and maybe even at any price) will do. Know what it is you are looking for instead of just going to a school because one of your friends or someone you know is going there. Know what it is that will make you stay there. Have clear objectives for what it is you want to accomplish. I know it's not always easy, especially now that you are maybe just beginning this new way of thinking, but the more you do it, the more comfortable you will feel and the easier it will become. In the beginning when you don't know anything, it is difficult, but as you continue in your profession, things will become clearer to you.

While we're on the subject of teachers, here's one of my favorite questions and something I advise you to look out for: Does your teacher *really* care whether you learn or not, or are they just happy that you signed up for the class so they get the cash? I'm lucky enough to have found a teacher who cares: Wendy Ward is the reason I decided to study the Meisner technique at the Ward Studio in New York. I had been shopping around, looking for the right school. When I interviewed her, I had a feeling that lasted a long time and finally led me to her studio a year and a half later. Right after I had talked to her for the first time, I wasn't able to attend her school because of time constraints. I was finally able to study with her and it turned out to be a good choice for me.

The same is true for all the other people you need on your team. These people will support you in your quest to become a successful artist. It is difficult to do many things alone in today's world. Look for good people, the right people, who can help you succeed.

Take Away

Who is on your team? What organization do you need to be successful? Do you need or have a manager, agent, good headshot photographer, publicist, résumé expert, career coach, teacher, acting coach, tax consultant, industry contacts? What's the team that will make you successful?

_____

_____

_____

9. Competencies

Another thing successful companies do is make sure that everyone in the organization can do their job. This is a two-step process; often the first step is given less importance, which can create difficulties later on down the road.

The first step in this process requires the identification of not only the technical skills necessary for employees in each position in the organization, but also their personality traits, mental attitude, the degree to which they are results-oriented, their ability to work alone if necessary and with others, leadership skills, good communication skills, and so on. The second step in this process is to select *only* those individuals who have the appropriate characteristics and traits.

For example, in my case, if I need motivation (and yes, sometimes I do too!), I go to Hollywood acting coach Bernard Hiller; for technical training, Wendy Ward; for coaching, Janice Hoffman or Leslie Becker; for head shots, Peter Hurley; when I need advice about TV hosting, I go to Pat Murphy-Stark; for help in navigating my way through the industry to get the results I want, I go to Brian O'Neil, and there are others. This is why your goal *must* be clear. If it isn't, you will have a difficult time feeling good about the people and things you put on this list, because it won't be very clear why you need them and how you would like them to help you.

Just as businesses do, you also want good results. You want to grow. You want to focus on the positive things and on the things that give you the return on your time and financial investments. That means you must surround yourself with good, positive, intelligent, and knowledgeable people.

Know what it is you expect of each person. Know what kinds of people you want to work with. Know what kinds of values, degree of professionalism, specific information you expect them to have for you, how you like to communicate and remain in contact with them, where you prefer them to be located, and so on. Be specific.

Take Away

Do you have every type of service on your list that you will need to achieve your goal? Do you know what you expect from each person on that list? Do you know what competencies and characteristics you want them to have and how you want them to interact with you?

Finally, the most important set of competencies to examine are your own. What competencies and skills do you need to achieve the success you want? Do you have them all? If not, what are you lacking and, most importantly, how are you going to ensure that you develop a particular skill?

---

10. Feedback, Coaching, and Developmental Plans

In order to ensure that everyone is in line with the mission and that everyone is really given an equal opportunity to perform his/her job well, companies set up an evaluation system in which the employee meets with his/her boss twice a year in addition to the regular feedback they receive on a daily basis.

During these sessions, the employee's overall performance is evaluated and strengths and weaknesses are highlighted. The strong points are applauded, and the weak areas are addressed in the form of a developmental plan. When the employee leaves that session, he/she will have specific tasks they must accomplish over time that will help improve performance. It is also the manager's responsibility to coach employees on a regular basis and to facilitate their learning.

I will elaborate more on this section than in some of the other business-related sections because I feel this is so important. Truly knowing yourself in any field is a big plus and such a huge help in achieving success. This means looking at yourself in the mirror and asking yourself if you have all the skills you need to achieve your goals.

This is an extension of the swot exercise, though it focuses on how to overcome your weaknesses and how to exploit your strengths. Even in your performing skills, you should be aware of what it is you need to work on. Make sure your teacher gives you the feedback you need. Demand it. If you're paying for those classes, you have a right to work in them just like you have a right to feedback. If you don't know where your weaknesses are, how can you improve them? Don't assume too much. Not everyone is in a position to evaluate himself objectively. Sometimes we need an outside, neutral point of view. Seek out and ask for qualified feedback and have the courage to accept the answer.

In my business as a corporate consultant, we sometimes use a tool that gives managers feedback from the people they work with. A third-party company provides a questionnaire that consists of some 200 questions that cover every area of a manager's ability to communicate, lead, direct, organize, work in a team, among other things inherent to that position. The manager receives a packet of questionnaires for himself to fill out and nine more for his boss, his colleagues at the same level, and for other colleagues he manages. All the questionnaires are sent directly to the company for processing by the individuals who fill them out. A few weeks later, the manager then receives a confidential report compiled of the participants' feedback about him. The only participants' names that appear on the report are his own and that of his boss. All the others are grouped together anonymously.

I then set up appointments with each manager who received the feedback to get his impression, his feelings, and to see how he feels about the others' perception of him. I have seen people cry during this phase. Some folks just aren't used to this type of feedback. Many people don't have a clue as to how the rest of the world perceives them, and it can be a rude awakening. Some then try to justify themselves on different points and say that they are not the way the others see them. I just respond, "Whether you think you are like that or not, that's the way they see you, and if that's the way they perceive you, then for them, that's the way you are. You can either accept that or not, but that doesn't change the perception."

I have been in classes in which the teacher gives us feedback, sometimes as a group but mostly individually. It is always interesting to see how people receive feedback. Some swallow it and take it in stride. Some find it difficult to accept and immediately try to justify themselves. Others find it too difficult to accept constructive feedback and they quit. Good, constructive feedback helps you get better. It's difficult to take sometimes, especially in front of your peers, but if it is taken to heart and applied, we can only reap the benefits.

We need to be more aware of ourselves. More importantly, when the competition is as stiff as it is, we need to be perfect. If the benchmark is to work continuously and to make a living from our craft, then we must be in the top percentile of our chosen fields.

Think back to the exercise we did at the beginning of the book, looking inside yourself and writing your life story. The more aware you can become of yourself, the more objective you can be in evaluating your potential. When you really know yourself, you know what you must do and you focus on self-improvement.

Take Away

How are you at accepting feedback? Do you seek out feedback regularly? Do you know what it is you need to work on to achieve greater success? If you do, what are you doing to ensure that you improve? Do you have a plan? Are you following it? Do you have a coach who is helping you with your career plans?

Do you have a regular acting coach or teacher you trust to give you good, constructive feedback?

---

11. Budgeting and Finances

A good business manages its financial situation very well. Having a budget and sticking to it are essential to overall business success. The budgeting process begins with the business plan. All spending can happen only if it is in line with the business plan. In other words, spending the company's money should always have to do with helping it accomplish its plan and ultimately achieve its vision. Managers get together and project what they will need to spend to achieve the company plan. Advertising, selling tools, computers, maintenance, and so on are all planned for and budgeted in advance. Once the general manager and finance director approve each manager's budget request, they will be expected to stay within that budget and save wherever possible.

Budgets are usually tight. That means there is little or no room for unplanned expenses. When I was in Nike, so many people asked me for sponsorships for their sons or daughters who played sports. My answer was most often no, because the company had a very clear strategy. It was to focus on the bigger teams that would get the company greater visibility. For the smaller teams and individuals, there were other programs that didn't necessarily include sponsorship but had other benefits to help improve their performance.

Do you know where all your money goes each month? I thought I did until some years ago when I monitored all my expenses over the course of several months. I kept and registered every receipt for every item I bought, whether it was a bottle of water, a taxi ride, a bag of chips, groceries, or whatever. I needed to do this in order to ensure that I wouldn't run out of money during my first year after having quit my corporate job. I knew that I would not be making much money during that year, and I wanted to make sure I budgeted accurately. If you haven't done it, I highly recommend it.

It is amazing to see how much we spend on Starbucks and cigarettes and other daily habits! While gathering information for my book, I was talking to a fellow actor who told me that sometimes he has to decide between paying rent and taking a class. If with better money management and a savings plan, even if just a few dollars a week, those kinds of decisions could be made easier for a lot of people.

Take Away

Do you know where your money goes? Do you monitor your spending on a regular basis? Do you have a budget? Are you following it?

---

12. Multitasking and Outsourcing

This concept is one that managers in today's business environment must be able to master. A friend of mine once took a job in a multinational company, and he was bragging about the compensation package he negotiated. I told him that if they are giving him a lot, they will be expecting a lot from him! Six months later, he told me that now he really understood what I meant. He said there were times when he didn't know whether he was coming or going. He had so many things to do, different projects to simultaneously manage, plus customers who needed his attention, employee problems to take care of, and so on.

The race is on and it is not just a question of who's the best but sometimes who can provide the highest-quality product or service the fastest. In order to do this, it is essential to surround oneself with good people and be able to manage multiple projects simultaneously. In some cases it might be necessary to find someone who can take care of a task, run an errand, develop a tool, or whatever.

Take Away

Could you be getting results quicker if you could do more things at the same time? Do you have a solid plan in place for when you need to get everything done? Are you organized? What do you find particularly difficult to manage? Where do you need help? Who can help you? Can you outsource some of your tasks?

---

13. Keeping in Contact with Customers

Staying in contact with customers and end consumers is of the utmost importance in business and is one of the most basic of all marketing principles. This is important for two reasons. One, it helps companies keep a pulse on the situation in the marketplace and lets them know what consumers need so they can be sure of creating the right products for the market. Second, consumers feel listened to and are assured that the company is interested in making products for them.

There are different ways to do this. Some companies conduct surveys and pass out questionnaires getting customer feedback in that way. Others hold focus groups, conduct events, provide product-testing opportunities, set up forums, discussion groups, ask questions online and encourage feedback, set up guest books to collect feedback. Still others just simply go out and talk with their customers one-on-one. Whatever the method, it is crucial to stay in contact, because only in this way can companies really know what their customers need and want and thus have a chance of making products that will sell.

Take Away

Do you know who your customers are? Are they casting directors, agents, and so on? Do you know what they are looking for? How often do you get out and talk to them? Do you have regular contact with your customers? What's your plan for keeping in touch with them? Is it working? If not, what will you change about it to make it work?

---

14. Marketing and Promotional Activities

Companies spend lots of money and energy on their marketing efforts. Obviously it is of little benefit to have a great product if no one knows about it. What's the point of having a great store, beautifully decorated, if you don't get any visitors? The best Web site is of little value if it receives no traffic.

There are countless ways that companies market their products—television, newspapers, magazines, and events. But things are changing. The effect of these mediums isn't what it used to be, which is pushing ad agencies and companies alike to think of new ways to reach their consumers. One of the ways that has grown in popularity over the years is the concept of giving: the more you give, the more you receive. This is why companies put out newsletters, e-books, offer free seminars, and give free samples, because statistics tell us that in the end, it pays off. Consumers today want to know before they buy a product that the company they are buying from is reputable, reliable, and credible. This is especially important for small businesses that are not known to the larger population or target audience.

If someone wants to sell something, they must market their product to their target audience.

Take Away

What methods are you using to market yourself as an artist? Are you getting the results you want? What could you be doing that you are not already? How many different ways are there to promote "you" and get recognized by your "customers"?

---

15. Growing the Market

Companies that have the power to innovate in a big way and create a following in the marketplace are the ones that don't concentrate all their efforts on taking market share away from their competitors. They don't spend all their time thinking about how to make sure they get a piece of the big pie. The most successful companies, the ones that have endured over the years, think about how to make the pie bigger! How on earth do they do that? The answer has to do with innovation and creating new products in new segments of the market that don't even exist yet.

There aren't very many companies that do this well, but those that do are raking in the bucks. Nike, Microsoft, and Google are some of the most obvious ones, but there are other small companies that do the same thing.

All this brings me to the concept of differentiation. For those who want to stand out from the crowd, it is essential that they be different from the rest in today's competitive marketplace. To do this, one must innovate. To innovate, one must do research, which is the next point on this list.

Building on the last section and what you are doing to promote yourself and answering the question, "How many different ways are there to promote 'you' and get recognized by 'your customers'?" challenge yourself to come up with an innovative idea to promote yourself in a way that is different from what others in your field are doing. I have a friend who has formed a production company. This is getting him greater visibility, which will be good for his business and will get him in front of people who are casting for movies and television, which is where he wants to work as an actor.

Take Away

What can you do that is different to promote yourself? What innovative ideas do you have to promote yourself? What resources do you have to promote yourself in a way that is different from your competition? Can you invent something that no one else is doing that will get you noticed and get your work on the desks of casting directors and agents?

---

16. Research and Development

In the last section we talked about being different in order to stand out in a very competitive environment. This requires innovative thinking to stay ahead of the game and ahead of the competition. It means being a leader and not a follower.

Companies invest large sums of time, money, and manpower on research and development, because they know it is of great value for their business's future. Taking time to figure out the evolution of market trends, what new products they can bring to market, pays dividends down the road.

Take Away

Are you doing regular research to keep abreast of what's happening in your market? Do you research and try new ways of doing things, promote yourself, study what successful people are doing, upgrade your knowledge on a continuous basis?

---

17. Sustainable Growth

Businesses make growth projections based on trends in the market, their ability to respond to what consumers need and want, and based on their plans. They try to ensure that over time, they will continue to grow. The last thing you want is to be blindsided because you weren't prepared. That is one of the big benefits of planning and research. Keeping abreast of what's happening and staying informed helps to reduce that risk, because you are prepared and can react in real time to any challenges that arrive.

The planning process is designed to ensure that the company will continue to grow over time. This is the concept of sustainable growth. To do this, it is necessary to have a long-term strategy.

Take Away

Is your strategy long term or short term? Are you thinking of what benefits you can get today, or are you setting yourself up for continued success? Are you planting the seeds for the future of your career? If so, how are you doing that specifically?

---

18. Technology

Keeping abreast of technological advances can be a huge challenge, but one that companies recognize as being important if they want to strive to achieve or maintain market leadership. Things change so quickly. Once it was important for businesses to have a Web site. Now there are many other considerations that stem from ways to provide consumers with newly updated content, building a list of people to market to, including audio and video and the ever-complex issue of search-engine optimization. The companies that are aware of these changes and keep themselves informed and react in real time are the ones that stay ahead of the game.

Take Away

Do you keep yourself on top of the technology game? Are you utilizing the most up-to-date techniques on the Web to promote your Web site? How can you use technology to promote yourself and keep in touch with your "customers"?

_____

_____

_____

19. Scorecard

One of the key elements to success in achieving goals is the continuous monitoring of efforts and of the plan. Many multinational companies use a process for monitoring their results called "the scorecard." This is basically a report card on how the company is doing with regard to its plan. There are periodic meetings, usually once a quarter, during which a group of senior managers sit around a table, discuss how they are doing against the plan, and grade their efforts. Questions are often asked as to what is working and what is not, why they are or are not on track in some areas, and what they must do to improve on poor results and maintain the good results they are getting.

Take Away

How often do you monitor your plan? Is your plan located somewhere that you can see it every time you come home so you can check your progress? What can you do to ensure you stay on track with focus and discipline?

_____

_____

_____

20. Increasing Shareholder Value

Public companies have a responsibility to themselves to be profitable and to deliver good-quality products. They also have a responsibility to take care of their employees, making sure they have what they need to successfully carry out their duties. Still another, very important responsibility they have is to their shareholders. These are the people who invest in the company. They invest in infrastructure, technology, and, mostly, in the company's stock. When people invest, they expect a return. If they don't get the return they hoped for, they pull their money out. It's that simple. You probably do the same when you invest in something.

Management is constantly concerned with increasing shareholder value, because if they can do that successfully and continuously, more people will invest and they can raise more money to grow the business.

Some of the things shareholders look for in the companies in which they invest are profit growth, increased sales, solid management team, good track record, innovation, and concern for the environment.

How does this relate to a career as an artist? There will always be people who invest in you as an artist. When agents send you out for an audition, he or she is investing their own credibility by betting that you will be prepared, on time, and give a good performance. Casting directors do the same when they send you to the producer for a screen test. Every time you come back with a positive result for them—you were on time, professional, gave a solid performance, responded to the casting director's requests for different monologues, scenes, and so forth—your stock price goes up in their eyes. When you don't do those things, your stock price goes down. You ultimately want to create value in your product in the eyes of those key contacts so that they will continue to invest in you. It's really all about being responsible and making their lives easier.

Take Away

What is your stock price with each and every one of your customers at this moment? What things do you do to increase your "stock price"? What do you do to create added value in your product?

21. Entrepreneurial Thinking

So now it's about taking all this information and putting it together to get your business of "you" going in the right direction, maintain your good results, or improve on others. Successful artists treat their careers as a business. They are the CEOs of their own companies. In my experience and research, I have formed my own idea of what it takes to be a successful business owner and entrepreneur. The following is a list of some characteristics that successful entrepreneurs have in common.

- Analytical skills
- Business skills
- Communication skills
- Curiosity
- Decision-making skills
- Discipline
- Drive and determination
- Flexibility
- Follow-through
- Hard work
- Honesty
- Innovation
- Love for what you do
- Money management
- Networking and relationship-building skills
- Objectivity
- Organizational skills
- Perseverance
- Physical & mental fitness
- Planning skills
- Positive mental attitude
- Resourcefulness
- Results-oriented
- Risk taker
- Self-confidence
- Sense of urgency
- Technical knowledge in field of choice
- Vision

Take Away

So do you have what it takes to manage your own career effectively to get exceptional results? If not, don't fret, because you have several options open to you.

First of all, lacking some of these characteristics doesn't mean that you can't be successful. There is no rule. What it means is that there is a stronger probability that you will take more time to figure things out, but your vision could still be possible.

You could get a career coach who can help guide you in the right direction. You could get a manager who will actually help you manage your career. If you recognize what it is you are lacking, then you could find help in those areas to develop your skills.

Below are some Web sites you could visit that might give you some insight about entrepreneurial thinking and setting up the business of "you."

www.jolten.com
www.actingcareerstartup.com
www.hendersonenterprises.com
www.successissweetest.com
www.organizedactor.com
www.actingasabusiness.com
www.businesstown.com/entrepreneur/index.asp
www.jumpstartcoach.com/top10.html
www.entrepreneur.com

So Now What?

Now it's about taking all this information and putting it together to get your business of you going in the right direction and to maintain your good results or improve on others.

If you need help with all this business stuff, there are many acting career coaches out there. Janice Hoffmann of successissweetest.com is one I know. I had her as a coach for six weeks as part of an intense summer acting program at the Ward Studio in New York. In this career-mentoring workshop, Janice basically took students through the process of goal-setting and achievement with the focus on acting. We concentrated a lot on knowledge of the market, creativity, and how to stand out and differentiate ourselves from the competition. I made more progress in those six weeks than I had in the prior six-month period, and I still have contact with Janice today.

Leslie Becker and Brian O'Neil are two others who have given me a wealth of information and coaching that has helped me get better results. I have personally had consultations with both and have taken Brian's all-day seminar. I highly recommend all three.

There are many coaches out there. I was lucky enough to find good people who are helping me further my efforts. If you need help, recognize it and go get it. If you are not achieving the results you want and as fast as you want, then you have two choices: continue doing what you are doing, asking people to help you and give you advice, spend time looking for answers and trying to figure things out yourself; or you can go to someone who knows the business and knows what it takes to be successful.

If you need to learn some business skills and how to apply them, you can head over to my Web site, www.actingcareerstartup.com to find coaching as well. I work with individuals and groups to aid in personal and professional achievement.

Remember this: what it's really all about is modeling successful behavior. There's no need to reinvent the wheel. There are actors who started out just like you and who are getting good results, and it's not always because they are better than you. It is often because they know how to conduct the business, which can make all the difference in the world. I have read several books that have many interesting tips, and while many are easy to read, they don't always tell you *exactly what you need to do* and how you need to do it. I am a step-by-step person. I like clear, precise explanations.

That's why in all my efforts in and outside of this book, on my Web sites, and in my seminars, I try and provide you that type of information so that when you leave me, you really understand and know exactly what you must do. If I'm not qualified or able to give you what you need because it's something I also need to know, then I will find someone who can tell both of us.

In my consulting and corporate training business, I see great trainers who keep trudging along, doing things the hard way, getting clients by word of mouth. Their businesses are small, and they make a modest living. Then there are the go-getters with lots of energy and innovative ways of doing things; they are not always better than the old dogs, but they are very good at the marketing game, and that makes a big difference. Those are the guys who make radio and television appearances, do interviews with the media, make audio CDs and DVDs, have Web sites that sell their products, have newsletters, collect names and addresses online of people they can market to, cross-sell, up-sell, do joint ventures, and have a host of marketing weapons they use regularly. When you add it all up, it pays off. Our business, your business as an artist, is subject to the same principles. You just have to know how to apply them. If you want people to notice you, if you want to stand out as an individual, no matter what you do or no matter what field you choose, you have to be good at marketing your product: YOU!

Putting It Into Practice:
A First Hand Account

JUST DO IT!

CHAPTER 13

Three Months in New York

This Is What I Did: the detail that you rarely ever hear from one person...

This part of the book is for Karen and all the young aspiring actors like her. I met Karen in Brooklyn on the set of the film *Life Support* (starring Queen Latifa) in Brooklyn for which we were both cast as extras. While I don't consider myself to be an expert on the business of acting by any stretch of the imagination, I have a great deal more information about this business than Karen, just as there are many actors out there who have a great deal more information than me. Karen is a beautiful young woman, who had driven through the night just to be on the set of this movie. She was so excited, and she talked about wanting to move to New York to seriously pursue modeling and acting. In the same breath, she confided to me, "I'm ashamed to admit it, but if I were to move here, I have absolutely no clue where to start and what to do about anything, getting an agent, working, networking, nothing!" We proceeded to talk at length, and she asked me a multitude of questions and took a lot of notes. I answered them based on my experience and what I had learned and put into practice.

I began to realize in these three months that I was "working the beat," that there are a lot of Karen's out there with a lot of questions, hungry for information, hungry for someone to take the time to explain to them what the possibilities are and to give them ideas as to what they could do to successfully promote themselves as young artists and, ultimately, to get work.

In my continuous quest for information, I've had many a conversation with working actors. I love to learn, so I pick their brains, ask a lot of questions. The problem is that rarely do those actors have the time to share with me all the details that I would like to know. There are the usual conversations in which all the typical questions are asked and answered: "What do you do? How long have you been acting? What have you booked recently? What agent are you with? Do they send you out a lot? Do you have your SAG/AFTRA cards?" But these are all very superficial questions. You rarely hear about all the *other* things a person does to promote himself or herself or what they did to land a part, the things that got them to that point.

Then this usually very busy person has to run before giving you the information that perhaps could of been of most value to you—how they market themselves, how they obtained that agent representation, and what their daily activities are that help them get frequent auditions and consequently book work.

That's what this section of the book is all about: getting down to the nitty-gritty of what it's like day to day; it's about stimulating thought, seeing the results one actor without much experience got during a three-month time span in New York, while applying what he has learned so far. Who is this actor? Me.

As I mentioned earlier, I want to make it clear that I am relatively new to the game. That's what makes this book's perspective different from a lot of books you read. Many books are written by so-called experts. I do not consider myself an expert at the business of acting. I do, however, know the basic principles of business, and I know how to apply them. But I'm still learning, and I'm still learning this business. I'm still training to become a better actor, and I have a ways to go.

I came to New York on a mission, and I achieved some results. Were they outstanding? No. Were they good? Yes. Could I have done better? Yes. Did I learn a lot? Hell yes! Will I be smarter going forward? You betcha!

I want to share with you all the details that you rarely hear from other actors. And while over the last couple of years, I have done independent films, commercial print work and industrials as an actor, in this section, I'm only going to concentrate on a particular three-month period, my goals, my strategy, my daily activities, how I networked, the classes I took. I'll tell you about my auditions—how I got them, what went well and what didn't, where I auditioned and for what and for whom. I'll show you how I kept track of them, kept statistics, analyzed them and made adjustments, how I began to build relationships and how I fared. And I'll talk about what I learned and what my next steps will be.

While you read this part of the book, I'm hoping that you will reason with me and my story, criticize my actions, praise them; think about what you would have done in my situation; make notes of similar things you think will work for you or things that I have done that you don't think will work for your situation; and think about what you feel I should do going forward. I hope that you will be stimulated to come up with variations of what I've done to fit your business. I hope to give you ideas and help you think of things that you maybe never thought of. All this I hope to do by exposing myself to the fullest. Why am I doing this? Because over the past year, I have listened to you and the many brand-new actors, and even those who have been around for a while, who have told me that this is the kind of information you need and want. I also hope to inspire other actors to share their stories as well. This way, we can all learn more.

I want to share my experience and in doing so, I'm expecting to get three different types of reactions from my readers.

The first will be from what I believe will be the smallest percentage of readers who pick up this book, people who might say something like, "Tony, you're not really talking about anything new. I do those things all the time and more. I'm already getting good results, and they are a lot better than the ones you are getting." The majority of this book probably isn't for that reader anyway. But that's okay, because I'm hoping they get something else of greater value from reading all this.

The second type of reaction I expect will go something like this: "Very interesting. Sounds like a lot of what I do, although I never knew that postcards (for example) could be used in that way." OR, "I should try doing cover letters like that too." OR, "I'm wondering why Tony didn't do such and such as well. I can't believe he didn't think about that too!" OR, "If I were him, I would advise him to do such and such. It's such a no-brainer!" These are the people who are similar to me and who might be happy to know that there are others like them out there with whom they have something in common. Nevertheless, hopefully they will be stimulated to think more about what they can do to promote themselves.

The third type of reaction I expect will be the biggest percentage of those who read this book, people like Karen, who told me that day on the set, "Wow! I never knew that there was so much to it! I had no idea that it was so much work! I'm going to some of those Web sites and start submitting myself right away. And…"

Whatever the reaction, my goal is to stimulate thought and to make you realize that it takes a lot of work to be successful. It will also help you understand that with dedication and hard work, one can get results.

Here goes…

As I have already mentioned, I have been living in Italy for the past ten years and periodically return to New York to pursue my acting and TV hosting dreams. If I were in New York constantly, it would be easier, but going back and forth is my current situation. I had planned to return to the Big Apple at the beginning of May 2006 to coincide with the beginning of the next level of my Meisner training. I would be there for three months.

I had worked well in my "other life" business—that of consulting and conducting seminars—and signed one of my biggest contracts to date in the spring of 2006. My business is growing. Since 2004 I have doubled my revenues. We're still small, but so far the business is serving its purpose of enabling me to make good money and put enough aside to come to New York to pursue what I really want.

I'm in the process of evolving that business and getting trainers on board to be able to conduct more open seminars, which will enable me to make more money with even less effort. That means I'll be able to spend more time to stay focused on my craft. But that's another book.

My Goals At The Offset

My goals were clear for that three-month period:

1.   Continue my Meisner acting training at the Ward Studio for the duration of the three months.

2.   Take a TV hosting class sometime during the three months.

3.   Start working/booking industrials, on-camera commercials, and commercial print work through an agent and online submissions.

4.   Get new color headshots. My headshots were two years old, and they were black and white. I knew the industry was moving to color, and I wanted to be in line.

5.   Finish writing my book.

6.   Give input to my webmaster for the revamping of my business Web site (Jolten Educational Events and Entertainment) so that I can begin collecting names for my courses and seminars this fall when I return to Italy. October 15 launch.

Preparing the Trip to New York

The plan began with mailings to my few contacts that I had made the last time I was in New York. Among the influential people in the industry that I had met were one casting director for industrials, one commercial agent, one commercial print agent who agreed to freelance with me, one TV hosting associate agent, and two producers who specialize in TV hosting whom I had met at a forum.

I sent them my two-year-old black-and-white head shot, a cover letter addressed to each individual that I had drawn up for every contact, and my résumé. In the letter, I specifically stated the reason why I was contacting them—to let them know that I was returning to New York (as they all had asked me to do) and to please consider me for any upcoming projects they felt I might be right for.

They all knew who I was, because even though I had met them almost a year prior to my writing these cover letters, I had kept in touch with them all via postcards that contained my picture and e-mail address. I wanted to stay on their minds and to keep them informed of my progress. I thought doing these mailings before my departure for New York would save me some time when I arrived. I wanted to hit the ground running.

Upon Arrival

When I finally arrived, I sent postcards letting them know I was in New York, and I called them. When I called their offices, I got the following unpleasant surprises:

The print agent I had been accepted to freelance with some months ago during my previous visit and who told me to keep her posted on when I would be coming back was no longer with the agency! I had been sending postcards for the last nine months to a person who wasn't even there! Do you think the agency would bother to contact me and let me know that? No! And that shouldn't be expected. It was my mistake to not stay informed. How could I have done that? There are different ways. *Ross Reports* and *New York Agencies*, for example, both usually list and update regularly all the agents and associate agents within each agency and sometimes even the assistants. Had I kept myself updated, I would have known that.

The exact same thing happened with my commercial agent. When I called, both the commercial print agent and the on-camera commercial agent's offices, I was told that since no one in the office knew me, I should send in my head shot and résumé and they would call me if they were interested. I had to start all over again! Neither office ever called me in, in spite of my efforts to contact the appropriate people via e-mail and postcards and by sending my headshot and résumé as instructed.

I was back at square one, without the agents I thought I had at the beginning of my three-month period. So much for hitting the ground running. Now I had to spend part of my already-brief three-month period looking for representation. Shit!

The industrial casting director, however, did call me back. She seemed very enthusiastic about calling me in for an audition for the right project. I was just happy that at least one of my contacts acknowledged me! I was hopeful.

Setting up Office

Since I wanted to maximize my time in New York, I started setting up office on day one. First I bought all the trade papers I thought I needed: *Backstage*,

Ross Reports, New York Agencies, Show Business, Casting Director Guide. It was probably overkill, as some of them have overlapping information, but I was gung-ho and wanted to have all the information in my office that I could possibly need.

I also went to the Actors Connection and picked up 100 envelopes with windows so that when I did my mailings, my headshot would be visible before the recipient even opened it up. They were expensive, but I thought it would be worth the investment. Always looking for ways to set myself apart from the rest.

I also got address labels for casting directors and agents. I knew they would make my job much easier. The labels contained the name and address of the agency or casting director's office, and the name of the contact person. They're a great way to save time.

In addition, I bought a portable stapler: résumés need to be cut to the exact size of the headshot and stapled to the back of it. We do it this way because agents and casting directors get so much mail. If your picture gets separated from your résumé, they might not find their way back together and may result in them both getting tossed out. Agents and casting directors are usually busy, and they don't have time to sort through the mess. I also carried around headshots and résumés with me all the time. You never know who you might meet or run into. One time I had gone to a seminar on a Saturday thinking that it would not be necessary to lug along all my stuff, so I left the headshot and résumé at home. I ended up running into a director for whom I had auditioned a few months prior, and he asked me for them again. I had to send them.

In the apartment I was subletting, I had my laptop with me but no printer. That turned out to be pretty costly, but I budgeted for Kinko's.

One of the first things I did was to get my résumé formatted in line with industry standards. I'm not going to spend time on that, but it is necessary. Again, we want to make it as easy as possible for agents and casting directors to read about us, to find the information they are looking for immediately without trying to figure it out. My résumé wasn't at all in line with the industry format. If you don't know what I'm talking about, inform yourself. There are many places for you to find out. As I mention later, Brian O'Neil's book has examples in one of the chapters.

What Happens When You Keep Your Eyes Open

In my first week I got a series of e-mails and newsletters from different schools, publications, and Web sites I had subscribed to. These usually free subscriptions are a great way to stay informed of what's going on in the industry, the types of classes offered, and many other things. One of those e-mails was from the Actors Connection. It was about two upcoming free seminars that they periodically have to promote other seminars and classes. These events are great places to ask questions and learn from the questions that others ask. One of the free seminars was about a program called the Conservatory, and the other was about a seminar called the Business of Acting, by a woman named Leslie Becker. I decided I would go.

I was familiar with the Actors Connection (www.actorsconnection.com) from my previous visits to New York. It is a great place to meet casting directors, managers, agents, and other industry professionals as well as to take classes and seminars. In some of their seminars, you can pay a fee to participate in a group question-and-answer session with the industry professional you choose from their brochure, and then you have a chance to do a monologue, a cold read, a commercial copy, or have a one-on-one interview. If I hadn't been a member, I might not have found out about the two free seminars.

The first one, about the business of acting, was exactly what I needed. I wanted someone to help me figure out exactly what I should do to get work and promote myself in the industry; even though I thought I had a pretty good idea, I still wanted someone with experience to give me a hand. Of course, the seminar was to stimulate interest in the four-week class, but it still provided us newbies with a lot of food for thought. I was excited about the content presented and what a class like that could do for me. I was also impressed with Leslie, with her many years of acting experience and the fact that she consults actors on the business side of their careers. I wanted to take her class, but the time was not good, as it was on the same night as my technique class.

The second free seminar was to inform actors about their AC Conservatory program, which was exactly what I needed! It had the following elements:

- One consultation with Leslie Becker
- Leslie's four-week class
- Another class of your choice
- Five Actors Connection seminars (where you get to meet one-on-one with casting directors, agents, and personal managers of your choice)
- An agent to send you out on auditions
- Discounts on some of their other classes and networking seminars
- I got to choose the start and end dates of this three-month program!

**This was the offer at the time. It may or may not be the same at the time you read this book.

I jumped at the chance to audition for acceptance into the program—I got an audition and was accepted. Finally, I was off to the races! I could have still been trying to figure out how to get representation, but now I already had it. Of course, there was a cost associated with this program, but I figured that if I got sent out enough, I would book something and make the money back. In the end, through all my efforts this summer, I did get work. So now I had an agent who promised to send me out on auditions. That would be great on top of what I already had planned to do.

Mailings? To Whom?

I figured that it would be wise to target my mailings instead of just sending them to every agent and casting director. I went through the *Ross Reports* and *New York Agencies and the Casting Director Guide.*

My goal was to target commercial agents, CDs (casting directors), and those who represent talent for industrials and print work. For agent mailings, I used mostly the *New York Agencies* to get names and addresses, because it gives a little bit more information, such as who the agencies' clients are, whether the agencies are union, whether they freelance, and, for me especially, whether they mention different ethnicities or certain age groups or types. In addition, there is a section in the front of the book that lists what some agencies are looking for in the month of that particular issue. I also found the names of the agents and associate agents that I needed to address in my cover letters.

I pulled out around thirty agents, wrote cover letters, used the labels to address the envelopes, and within the first two days, sent out that first mailing.

Then I did the same thing with casting directors. I targeted both commercial CDs as well as those who cast for industrials (projects done for corporate accounts). Industrials could be video presentations for their internal or external clients, live events, and so on.

In the many Q & A sessions I had attended with casting directors and from my conversations with them, I learned that the really busy directors don't call in much talent from mailings, but rather work with trusted agents to get the talent they need.

Just a word about the cover letters. Some of the Web sites I suggest later on will help you format your cover letters. One thing I learned over the past couple of years is how important it is to be clear, concise, and to the point. Remember that the people you are sending your cover letter to have a lot of mail to read. The four major components of my letters:

1.   A brief introduction of myself and why I was writing the letter

2. How I could "make their job easier" (for casting directors I actually used those words)

3. Inform them of what I was doing at the time I wrote the letter (acting jobs, callbacks, training, etc.)

4. Call to action: let them know that I would like an appointment or that I would call them or ask to be called in

Since my headshots at the time were in a horizontal format, I formatted my cover letters to about one third the normal 8 x 10 format and stapled them to the front of the headshot, to the right of my face. Again, this way the people reading my mailings would have all the information they need at one touch. This was one of the many little tips I learned from Leslie Becker.

One morning about two weeks later, I received a call from the office of a producer I had met a year before and with whom I had kept in touch. The voice on the phone said they were looking for someone who could help them complete a project for one of their clients. She said her boss just laid my headshot and résumé on her desk and said, "Call this guy. Maybe he can do it." It was a program on the Learning Channel in which I was to play a speech therapist being interviewed. She sounded desperate and said they needed me to come in and tape it that very afternoon and asked if I was available. I jumped at the chance and remember thinking, "These mailings are starting to work!" Mass mailings became my activity every three weeks. I also did spot mailings using postcards to say thank you to casting directors for having me into their offices or for calling me to do extra work.

Aside from those unsolicited mailings, I also checked *Show Business* on Tuesdays, *Backstage* on Thursdays, and a series of casting Web sites (I'll list them shortly) to see if there was anything I should submit for. My submissions were always in line with the instructions on the breakdowns (the page with the project's name, the pay scale, the roles, the descriptions of what casting directors are looking for, and the submission instructions), regarding where to send photos and résumés. Some CDs prefer that you stay in touch via e-mail, regular post, and many often request that you print the name of the role you're submitting for on the front of the envelope. Sometimes, for really important projects or for ones that require that the submission be received immediately, I do a drop-off at the casting director's office. Some offices have a bin right outside the door in which actors can leave their materials.

One thing that's good to know is that the casting for some projects must happen at lightning speed. I've been told that by the time you see a casting notice in a trade paper, it could already be too late to submit. Castings for TV move much faster, so consider doing a drop-off just to make sure your materials get to the right person in time.

So the first mailing was always the headshot, résumé, and a personalized cover letter. For subsequent mailings to the same people, I used postcards to update them on my progress. I always set aside a few mornings or late nights to write the cards. It wasn't a job I particularly enjoyed, but I believed it to be necessary. A bit later we'll talk about the results I obtained.

Putting the Team Together

Just as I talked about in the business concept section of this book, I wanted to assemble a small team of people to help me get the best possible results for these three months and for my future. One of these people would be my agent, who would send me out on auditions. I decided to go to the Actors Connection and try and meet some other agents with whom I could possibly freelance. I also needed some expert business advice on how best "to move" in the industry, with tips and suggestions that are specific to my case. This is the team I came up with.

Agent # 1

My agent/manager, who will remain anonymous, as that person is part of the Actors Connection program, was doing a great job getting me auditions. Aside from that, she is a great person, a delight to work with and has great respect in the industry. Also her staff is very professional and pleasant to work with. I'm showering them with compliments, not only because I mean every word I wrote, but because for me it's important to work with people that I like.

Agent # 2:

I also met another agent at the Actors Connection. During my five-minute, one-on-one session with her, I read my commercial copy and chatted with her. She told me, "You have a great look, and I believe you are very marketable." Then she made me smile when she moved closer as if she didn't want anyone else to hear, even though we were alone, and said, "I don't usually say this to very many people at events like this, but I would call you in tomorrow for an audition. I really think you'll book something."

I thought, "That is a nice thing to say, but show me the money. Send me out on something. I'm available." She called me the next week for an audition and over a six-week time period, she called me in about four times. Doesn't seem like much, but those four were in addition to the other auditions I had been on. Every audition is another chance to book some work. At any rate, she was one of the nicest people you ever want to meet.

Just a side note here. While we're on the subject of finding industry professionals who are interested in you as an artist, I must say that I also met a good number of agents and casting directors at some of those seminars, who didn't seem interested in me at all. While that's not what you want to hear or feel, that's part of the game.

You can freelance with as many agents as you want. Just be careful because if you have too many different agents working on the same kinds of projects and submitting you for the same types of jobs, you could end up having to choose.

Fortunately, this happened only twice in the three months I was in New York. Once, one of my agents called me for an audition gave me all the details about where to go, what time and what my role would be, and I confirmed that I was available to go. Then, about two hours later, my other agent called to offer me the exact same project, the exact same audition. At that moment, I was glad I had made clear to both agents that I was freelancing with different people, so when I told him that I had already been invited to that audition, it was no problem. It was first come, first serve.

Business Mentor #1

One person I wanted in my corner was Brian O'Neil. I had read his book *Acting as a Business*, which is one of the most-read books among actors today. After reading it, I understood why. I took a seminar with him and decided to talk with him one-on-one about my situation and see if he had any valuable advice for me. Of course, he did. Aside from his interesting and unique perspective on how to build an acting career, he gave me some very valuable tips and helped me iron out a plan with which to position myself for success the next time I come to New York

Business Mentor # 2

I also visited Leslie Becker for a personal consultation. Although I couldn't take her class because of scheduling conflicts, I was glad I saw her. She listened well, which is what a good coach does, and she gave me a lot of valuable advice. At our meeting's end, we had laid out three specific goals for me to achieve over the following two months.

Personal Manager

I met another personal manager at the Actors Connection who expressed a great deal of interest in me. She said she would call me into her office for an interview the following week. She kept her word. What she told me was music to my ears: She talked about managing my career and that she wasn't interested in the short term. She wanted me to grow, and she wanted us to grow together. She told me to get new head shots, which I had planned to do anyway, and she wanted to help me pick them out. She thought I would be good for *Law & Order* one day and wanted to groom me for that (my dream job!). She said she wanted to freelance with me for a few months first so that we can see if we are right for each other; then, if all went well and we were both happy, we could sign a contract. While I thought this was a great idea, I was also honest with her about my situation and that I would be leaving the country for a while. She said to keep in touch and that we could possibly start working together when I got back. In the meantime, she would submit me for any projects that came up for which she thought I was well suited.

A Teacher and a Coach

Two other people on my team are my acting teacher, Wendy Ward, and my coach, Janice Hoffmann. They are both a source of inspiration and provide very direct feedback, which I like. I can always bounce ideas off them and get their opinions, which I value a great deal. Both have been a tremendous support to me throughout this book project. They are good people to have in my corner.

A Good Friend

And last but not least, there's Laura, who wrote the Preface. She has years of experience, and her feedback and suggestions are usually spot-on.

So that's my team for starters. Down the road, I will surely add more people.

Which Acting Technique Is Right for Me?

I started out with what I believe to be method-based acting, but I didn't feel it and I wasn't getting the results I wanted fast enough, so I began asking myself if there were other techniques and methods that I might find easier and that might give me more immediate results.

I knew of Lee Strassberg and Stanislavsky. I knew of Stella Adler and her method. I had read about Ute Hagen and about Sandford Meisner. There are probably other methods and techniques as well that I'm not aware of. With this level of experience, I truly felt that at some point it becomes necessary to incorporate a little of all the different techniques to be a really good actor. I might be wrong, though. I can see some acting teachers reading this and cringing and saying, "What is he talking about?"

I chose Meisner and I like it. It's good to know what you feel most comfortable with and that you feel comfortable with the teacher and feel that she is giving you what you need to be a better actor. I have my criteria for choosing a teacher that I shared with you earlier.

I have seen some actors give up or get frustrated, because they're not progressing like they want to. There certainly could be a lot of different reasons for that. We are all different. One thing that I would take into consideration before being too hard on yourself, is another teacher and another technique.

Acting Training

I continued my studies at the Ward Studio on 28th Street. I had begun the program last year and was very happy with it. This time, taking the class was different. Last year when I was here, I went through an intensive, as I mentioned at the beginning of this book. There were voice, movement, and text for auditions, and Shakespeare, Meisner technique, and career mentoring. There was always something to do for one of the classes. We rehearsed in the evenings, on weekends, late at night—whenever was necessary. This year, I chose to take the technique class plus some other more technical classes, such as hosting, business, and voice-over.

This time it was more difficult to focus. When I came to class, I always had other things on my mind that I had to clear out first. Plus when you are totally immersed in a program, it has a stronger effect. I would suggest to any new actor, even if you don't have a lot of money for a conservatory-type program, to spend at least several weeks in which you totally dedicate yourself 24/7 to an acting program intensive. It's great to be able to concentrate fully on your craft and try to improve every part of it.

This time, for these three months, we worked on emotional preparation and choices. Great exercises. I definitely need more of that.

Auditioning

In the meantime, I started getting called out on auditions, mainly for commercials but also for castings and "go-sees" for some print work. I was psyched to audition; commercial auditions are often about improvising. For example, in one audition, I was asked to imagine that I was a CEO who woke up in the middle of the night hungry. So he goes to the kitchen and has to look for the bread and peanut butter and jelly to make a sandwich, but he's not familiar with his own kitchen, because he has a housekeeper. I had to completely create the kitchen in my mind and really look through those imaginary cabinets until I found what I was looking for.

On another commercial audition, together with a female actor, we had to mime like we were getting out of a car and stepping onto the red carpet of an awards ceremony. We had to stop and pose for pictures.

On still another audition I was simply asked to tell them a little about myself as they were more interested in the personality of the talent they were to hire. I learned there that it's good to have ready a presentation speech that is crisp, clear, concise, and that maybe tells a little story (a technique I learned in Pat Murphy-Stark's TV hosting class) that will help set you apart from the rest of the pack. In that audition, I told the following story:

> *"Potrei parlare italiano, oder Ich koennte auch Deutsch sprechen, but I don't think that speaking Italian or German for this audition is probably the right thing to do right now, so I'll continue in English. I did, however, live in both of those countries for many years during my fourteen years in Nike and Levi's. My time in Nike was particularly enjoyable and interesting. To give you an idea of that, I'd like to tell you a little story.*
>
> *One day, at the beginning of my career in Nike, I was called into my boss's office, who was the sports marketing manager. He asked me what I had on my schedule for the following week. "Nothing in particular," I answered. "Why do you ask?" He said he wanted me to go to the BMW dealer first thing on Monday morning to pick up the brand new 850i that he had ordered and then go with him to the airport to pick up Michael Jordan. He wanted me to be Michael's personal escort and translator for the week during his promotional visit to Germany.*
>
> *That is just an example of how cool it was for me to work for that company. But years later, I had to strive for my dreams, and even though it was difficult breaking off my employment, I left Nike to found my own company that would give me the time as well as the financial flexibility to pursue acting and TV hosting. And that's why I'm here now."*

My story must have worked, because I got the job! Telling a story was just one of the many tips I got from Pat's class.

What's Working and What's Not

At one point, after about twelve auditions and castings and without getting one callback, I realized I should probably take an on-camera commercial class.

While some actors tell me that twelve auditions without a callback is common, I still began to wonder if there was something I could do to better my chances.

To analyze your situation, it is necessary to keep good records. I used Leslie Becker's book *The Organized Actor* to keep track of all my auditions. In her book are audition pages in which you can log everything about an audition, such as role, location, name of CD's office, time, wardrobe necessary, materials to prepare, comments, among several other things. I used this tool faithfully and periodically go back and analyze my situation.

One of the things I looked at, were the roles for which my agent submitted me. I looked at this because sometimes at auditions I felt out of place or not right for the part they were casting. I also thought about my ability to improvise and decided I needed to work on that. However, I was already enrolled in other classes and had many other things going on, so I opted not to take an improv class right away. Instead I looked at other things I could improve on.

In the seminars at the Actors Connection a year ago, I was up in front of commercial casting directors; they complimented me on my read but told me to be more natural and a little less "over the top." They said the read of the commercial copy should be very conversational, like I'm talking to my friends. They said this is because of the effect reality TV has on everything. Commercials today are often about real people and not some actor or spokesperson, as was the case many years ago. I reflected back on those auditions of the previous year for which I was not called back and tried to remember if I was conversational and natural. I decided that that was something I needed to be conscious of.

I'm sure you've guessed by now that I am very determined. I sometimes walk around my house while doing something and say to myself, "I'm gonna make it! I'm gonna get what I want!" I would say this several times a day. Every time I went in for an audition, I would tell myself, "You have to book this!" In this first analytical phase, I wondered if my behavior was too aggressive. What you bring to a scene can help you make it more real, and certain emotions can influence how the scene comes off. I wondered if feeling that I needed to succeed at all cost was hindering my chances of booking the job. I decided I needed to relax.

To help me with that, I followed the advice of my acting teacher and read *Zen in the Art of Archery.* I immediately understood why I should read it. She, too, saw in me this desire to succeed at everything I do, and while that can be a healthy attitude, it's not good if it's too much and comes out as aggression or over-the-top determination while I'm acting.

Finally, I decided that I needed to arrive at the auditions earlier than I had been, get dressed (in ninety-degree heat, it is almost impossible to arrive at the audition without being drenched in sweat, so I always took clothes with me and changed there), get the copy, really master it, and then sign in at my call time. Maybe that would help me to relax even more.

One day I talked to another actor, Clark Beasley, whom I had met about a month prior and run into again at a voice-over audition. (You often see the same faces at auditions!) I was feeling down that day, and fortunately I ran into him. Even though we had met before, we never really talked much. We spoke for a half hour, and he gave me a pep talk, telling me that when he started out, it was the same for him and that one day things will just start to click. "You'll see," he said.

One Helluva Week!

Monday

When I arrived home that day after my conversation with Clark, my agent called and said I had just booked an industrial! It was actually the first of three auditions I had had that day. The job would be a half-day shoot for New York Life. It wasn't a whole lot of money, but it did wonders for my ego! Then, just minutes later, I got another call from my agent's office saying that I had been called back twice—for Pfizer and for a Mercedes-Benz on-camera commercial. Great!

You can imagine how my mood changed in just a period of a few hours.

That same evening, a photographer called me. I had done a submission on NYCastings. He said he saw my pictures and really liked them. They were 95 percent sure they wanted to use me for a stock photo shoot, but just to make sure, they wanted me to meet them in New Jersey. They would pay me and give me the pictures of the shoot. That was great, because I had just been thinking of getting a comp card made up. (Comp cards are what models and print talent send out instead of just a headshot. It gives different looks and usually consists of four to five photos, plus the model's measurements.)

Wow, I was on a roll!

Decisions, Decisions

So all that happened on Monday. So far, so good.

Tuesday

On Tuesday I had two auditions in the morning, one of which was the Mercedes callback. I did what my agent told me and wore the same clothes and did the same thing I did on the first audition as much as possible. This is pretty standard and is because when they saw you last time, they liked what they saw. I felt it went well and was pretty confident.

That afternoon I went to see the photographer. They snapped a few shots of me for their files and confirmed me immediately for three days' work! My first day was Friday of that same week. The photographer said that it was easy to get the shots he needed from me in just a short period of time and that he was surprised how many people come to castings and who say they have experience but who can't even take simple adjustments to take natural photos.

Late Tuesday afternoon, I was called by a noted casting director's office to come in and audition for an on-camera commercial I had submitted for. I was psyched about that audition, because they were looking for an actor in my age range who had a "doctor look," and who would be able to handle reading a lot of copy. I confirmed that I would be in for the audition.

Wednesday

That audition was on Wednesday. I got there a half hour early. Got dressed. Looked sharp. I even bought some eyeglasses at Duane Reade for $10 to complete my doctor look; I had often heard that one should at least try to wear clothes that speak to the role. I got the copy and went over and over it until I felt really comfortable.

I nailed that audition! It was for a company called Iovate. I was to be a doctor giving a presentation to a lot of people. The shoot was to be in Toronto, Ontario, and the pay was extremely decent. I felt so good about what I did. The casting director told me, "That was a very nice read, and I hate to be superficial, but the look is great. I'd just like you to read it again for me and do it with a little bit more of a smile and warmth toward your audience." I did that and the two people in the room seemed very pleased; they also complimented me on my second take and again on my look.

Just a little side note here: When I talk about the people in the room during the audition, often there is someone in the room who works in the casting office and who simply has the responsibility to make sure that the actors' auditions get put on camera and saved for their client to see. I don't always put a lot of stock into their opinion, even if it's positive, because I don't know how much decision-making power they actually have in the casting office. As a matter of fact, I try not to focus too much on the feedback. I just like to forget the audition as soon as possible and move on, not thinking whether or not I get the job. When I get a callback or get put on hold, that's a different story. I'd be a liar if I said I didn't think about it.

In this particular audition for Iovate, one of the people in the office was a middle-aged man who wasn't working the camera but who seemed to have a more important role. That made me feel even more confident. He was the one giving me most of the feedback.

I felt good, and for the first time, I was sure I would get called back. Later that afternoon, I received a call from my agent telling me that I have been put on hold for the Mercedes commercial! The dates were Friday of that same week for a fitting and Monday and Tuesday of the following week for the shoot. The pay was okay—about $500 per day plus residuals. (Depending on how often the commercials are shown, sometimes the actors receive checks periodically. This also depends on the type of contract.)

Thursday

On Thursday morning I got a voice mail from the casting office asking to put me on what is called a "first refusal" for the Iovate commercial. That means that I was in the running and that they were in the process of choosing between the finalists. To my knowledge, it's very similar to being put on hold. Of course, they wanted to know if I would be available to shoot. The dates were Tuesday and Wednesday of the following week. Shit! That job overlapped with the Mercedes job by one day.

Having a sense of moral obligation and integrity and at the same time driven by my hunger for both these jobs, I took a very real and honest approach and weighed the possibilities. How could I do both? I called my agent to see if she had heard anything from the casting people for the Mercedes project. She had not and said that in answering my other questions, it was entirely possible they would call the day of the fitting to tell me where I needed to be and at what time. She did say, though, that she would try and get some information. I learned from some of my actor friends that it was also possible they would decide not to use me and not even call me to release me from hold status.

What could I do to make sure I got at least one of them? I called some of my actor friends to ask for advice. No one was available. I was buying time, but I had to call him back! I decided it was best to just tell the truth to the Iovate casting director. I told him that I was already on hold for Mercedes and that I would still love to be taken into consideration for Iovate. I had to leave him a message, though, as he wasn't available to talk.

Then I remembered that I had the photo shoot the next day! What should I tell the photographer? I couldn't just expect him to stay on standby for me. What if the Mercedes people called me today and told me they wanted me tomorrow? What if they called me on Friday during the photo shoot?

Again, bound by my sense of moral obligation, I called the photographer Thursday morning and told them the truth. Even though I had already mentioned to him the day before that I had been put on hold, I told him that I still hadn't heard anything and but that it was possible I'd get called out during the shoot.

He appreciated my candor and was very understanding. He told me that they really wanted me for the shoot and that without me it wouldn't be the same. I was really moved by this. He said that I should come anyway at 9:00 a.m. If I got a call to go to Manhattan for the fitting, he would personally take me to the ferry (the shoot was in New Jersey) to make sure I got there on time.

I was so thankful, because I fully realized that I could possibly lose all three of those jobs! At least I was sure I had one!

Disappointed, Happy, and Grateful

Friday

I got up bright and early and went to the photo shoot, which went well. By lunchtime, however, I still hadn't received a phone call from anyone about anything I had been put on hold for. I was angry and very disappointed that I didn't at least receive a phone call releasing me from hold status. After all, I knew that being put on hold doesn't mean that you will book the job, but I had given my word to be available for those dates and in this case, I even turned down another job (as I was not sure that I was on hold for the Iovate commercial). All I asked for was someone to have the courtesy to give me a call and say, "Thanks anyway." Nothing!

By early afternoon, I called my agent and asked if she had heard anything. She had not and said that at that point it was safe to assume that I was released. I then called the CD for Iovate to tell him that news, and he, too, said that I had been released from that project.

Wow! What a week. What a seesaw ride from one week to the next. So, how did I feel? Disappointed that I didn't book one of the commercials. Disappointed that they didn't release me officially. Happy that things were starting to happen and that people really are interested in me and that the adjustments I made in my auditioning seemed to have produced results.

I was grateful that at least I got something out of it all—a photo shoot with a very understanding photographer on a paying job that will give me some great photos for my comp card. Now I don't have to pay another photographer! So all in all, it was a pretty good week. Still, I would have liked to book one of those commercials! It's just a matter of time and I know I will.

In talking to my actor friends, they complimented me on getting the call-backs and for getting put on hold. The also told me that the longer I do this, the more weeks like this I will have. I will get put on hold, and then dropped; I'll book jobs, and I will have decisions to make about which job to take. So, they told me, I'd better get used to it.

BEWARE!

Here are two stories that I hope you never experience yourself one day.

Is That Normal Practice?

The first story is about an agent I encountered and had met from a mailing I did. He called me one day and said he had seen my head shot and asked me to come in and meet with him. Of course I said yes, although I started to detect a bit of sarcasm and surliness in his voice.

When I arrived in his office, he was very hurried and not very polite. He asked me for my headshots. I was ready but wondered why he didn't have the one I sent him. He looked at them and told me point blank that "they look like shit" and that he wouldn't be able to get me work with those pictures. He told me what kind of photos he wanted and then said something that made an alarm go off in my head. On a small piece of paper, he wrote the name and telephone number of a photographer he wanted me to use to get new head shots. Hmmm. He also told me to bring the contact sheets (the pages with all the pictures taken at the shoot, or at least the best ones) so that he could help me choose the best ones to market myself.

Well, I went to get new headshots, but I didn't go to the photographer he suggested. I had one already chosen. When I called him back, he didn't seem to remember me at first. I explained that I had gotten new head shots like he suggested, and he immediately asked me who took them. I told him the photographer's name and he blurted out, "Why didn't you go to the photographer I told you to go to?" I told him, "Because I already had my photographer, and I preferred to go to him. The pictures are good." He snapped back, "Let me be the judge of that!" I had no intention of going to his photographer out of principle. I'm not here to feed his business; I'm looking for an agent who is really interested in working with me. As long as the pictures are good, what does it matter where I get them?

I just imagined him telling me that the pictures were no good and that he wanted me to go get the others. But here's the funny thing. I must have talked to seven different people about this particular agent, usually starting out with the question of whether or not they ever heard of him. I swear I got five identical answers: "Oh God, stay away from him." I met two young women, both in their late twenties, who told me they first had to get the pictures from the recommended photographer, and then they had to pay to get into his "book" that he presumably uses to sell his clients to his casting contacts. One girl told me about an agent she works with for print and told me all the things I just told you. I thought to myself how familiar that sounded; then I asked her who the agent was. It was the same person! Wow!

I'm telling you this to let you know that things like that can happen. I don't think that requiring a client to use a specific photographer or having clients pay to be inserted in a book are normal practices. I might be wrong, but I don't think so. On the other hand, one could argue that paying to meet casting directors is along the same lines. I'd rather pay to meet a casting director face-to-face, especially when 95 percent of agents don't ask for their clients to pay to be inserted in a book (at least to my knowledge).

Foul Audition

The second little episode has to do with an audition I was invited to one Saturday afternoon. I had worked on a film as an extra one day in late June. In all the downtime, I was sitting there talking to Karen when someone touched me on the shoulder. He told me he was a producer/director who was here that day with his wife and daughter, who were doing extra work. He said he thought my look would be good for a future project he was working on and that he was holding auditions that Saturday. When he asked if I would like to come and audition, I said yes and thought that this is one of the reasons I wanted to do extra work right now, because of the possible contacts.

However, I wondered how legit this guy was. He had told me that the audition announcement was in that week's *Backstage*. I checked and it was. I was excited that someone had actually asked me to come and audition personally because of who I was and what I transmitted to him. When I arrived at Ripley Greer Studios on 8th Avenue that Saturday afternoon, I saw a young woman who seemed to be coming from the same audition I was going to. I asked her if she had been to the audition and she said that she had. I then asked her how it went. She told me that she didn't stay to audition. When I asked her why not, she told me that they were asking people to sign a release form for the use of the audition tapes as well as the actor's "life story." That sounded very peculiar. She handed me the form and told me I could have it, because she didn't need it anymore. I thanked her and read the form. I couldn't believe what I was reading.

It basically said the actor grants their production company permission to use the audition tapes in any way they choose and that the actor's image could be freely used in association with different types of programming. In addition, by signing this release form, the actor gives all power to this production company and exempts them from any legal action that might result from the materials provided (the tape) from this audition. The production company also said it had the right to delve into the actor's personal life story and use that information for the programming.

I then saw another girl come downstairs. She immediately pulled out her cell phone. I couldn't help but overhear part of the conversation. It sounded like she was on the phone with her father, telling him that she just got out of the audition but that she didn't stay because they asked her to sign a release form. I talked to her after she got off the phone and she was relieved. Her father told her she had done the right thing. She was twenty-one years old.

Since the producer had asked me personally, I still went up to the audition. When I arrived, his wife was in the reception room. She had been there the day I met her husband while she and her daughter were doing extra work. She gave me two different forms to fill out along with the form I had already seen from the girl downstairs. I asked her if it was obligatory to sign the form. She said she wasn't sure and that it would be best to talk to the director.

I was asked to go into the audition room together with another woman. When I entered the room, the producer I had met was there with his brother, whom I also met that day on the set. I immediately asked if it was obligatory to sign the release form in order to be auditioned, because I told him that I couldn't sign it. His brother tried to explain to me that it was just so they had permission to give this material to casting directors and to market me. Hmmm. I told him I understood, but that if I were to sign it, we would first have to change the wording. The director told me that it was no problem, which I understood to mean that I could audition anyway. He was polite in telling me that without that signature, he could neither audition me nor take my picture and résumé. I stuck to my decision and turned to leave. He then asked me if I would stay and read the other part for the girl who went in with me. I jumped at the chance. I wanted to satisfy his curiosity and show him what he was missing!

He asked me to stay and read for the next woman who came in as well and I did. It was a comical part, and I was having a ball with it. The five people who were in the room were laughing, so I felt like I was doing what they asked me to do.

That was it. Never heard from them again, nor did I search them out. It was an interesting experience, and I felt good that I stuck to my decision. My instinct told me that it would have been wrong to sign that paper. I just believe that I didn't need to sell myself out for any type of job that I might have had. I have pride and I decide how interested I am to do a job, first and foremost.

Extra Work

Karen asked me once, "What are the different roles that one can interpret in a film or on TV?" There are several roles: leading, contract; supporting; featured; recurring (appears regularly in smaller roles on the program); day-player (needed for one or more scenes on the same day); under-five (under five lines); featured extra (extra who's placed in a specific place during a scene, no speaking lines); and extra (no speaking lines).

I had contacted casting directors who specialize in extra work and was called by a few of them. Usually there was a call just the day or even the evening before asking if I was available the next day early in the morning.

Once I was called on a Sunday afternoon. I had company from out of town and had taken them to see a Broadway show. At 5:00 p.m., when we exited the theater, I found a voice mail on my phone asking me to call this particular casting director. They asked if I was available to work on "a TV show" with Timothy Hutton and if I could be there the next morning at 7:30 with a tuxedo. I didn't have a tux! I left it at home in Italy! I didn't even think that I would ever need a tux! So I called and told them that I didn't have a tux but that I would try and find one. The person on the other end of the phone told me that that was fine and if I found one to let him know. I spent an hour and a half in a store trying on tuxedos, but they were too sloppy-looking. As I was there, I realized I didn't know exactly what the tux was for. What kind of scene was it? Was it a drama or a morning show? I didn't know! Damn! I was kicking myself in the ass! I was thinking that if it was for a morning show, I would have to be really sharp. It would have to fit me perfectly, because I could be standing there more like a model and have to look good.

On the other hand, if it was for, say, a party scene, maybe the fit wouldn't be so crucial. Of course, it couldn't be baggy, but maybe I could get by with something a little less form fitting. At any rate, I wasn't happy with the fit. It looked terrible, and there was no time to have it altered, nor did I want to, because I had every intention of taking it back the next day. However, I wanted to make a good impression and not show up looking like I had no eye whatsoever for fashion. So I called back and told them I didn't have a tux. They said they would call me again soon. And they did.

The very next week, they asked me to dress like an FBI agent. At first I thought, "Oh, that's easy. Coat and tie and we're in." Then I thought, "But what kind of coat? What color? How many buttons? What kind of shirt and tie would an FBI agent wear? What kind of collar on the shirt? What kind of hair-cut? So I went and visited the FBI Web site and looked up their dress code, which had explanations and pictures and everything. I was just trying to be as truthful as I could, even as an extra.

I look at it this way. If I'm a director and am working with extras, would I prefer to work with actors who "get it"? Actors who come well prepared and to whom I could upgrade to a speaking role if necessary? Or would I rather work with someone who just shows up? The answer was clear to me, so I tried giving the directors what they were looking for. Therefore, I had shirts with different collars and had a white shirt that fit the bill. I also had a jacket and tie that was right. But I still needed a jacket that I could wear in lieu of a suit jacket, so I went to another well-known store in southern Manhattan and bought a jacket that I would take back the next day.

Wearing that jacket on the set got me a lot of points. The wardrobe people liked it so much, that they asked me to appear in places where I was extremely visible. Two days later, I took the jacket back to the store and got my money back. Having said all this, I should mention that most of the time, or so I've been told, they have everything you need in their own wardrobe department on the set, especially on big-budget productions.

Personally, I don't find extra work to be the most interesting, to-die-for work in the world, but I want to be able to say that I've done it. Some people do it for a living and some do it between jobs, because they have to do something to make money. Right now I decided to do it for the experience, to learn and to meet people who can help me further my career and to meet other actors, directors, casting directors, and staff. I wanted to learn as much as I can. If you ever do extra work, though, make sure you take along a good book to read. If you don't, you'll wish you had!

It's Interesting

When you do extra work, there's a lot of downtime and waiting around. There's a room called "Holding" where all the extras wait until they're called for their scenes. There's plenty of time for small talk, but it's also a great time to pick the brains of some more experienced actors. They are also great moments to interview new actors if you're thinking about writing a book specifically for them!

Some actors told me that their agents don't want them doing extra work. Some say it's because it might ruin their image. Some say that once you are known for doing extra work, it is difficult for people to see you any other way.

The holding area is divided into sections for SAG (Screen Actors Guild) members (on SAG films) and Non-SAG members. This doesn't mean that one is better than the other or that one has better furniture or is more comfortable than the other, but there are definite class distinctions.

For example, there is usually a table or an area where you can find snacks, bagels, drinks, and so forth. At lunchtime there is a strict order that must be adhered to. First the crew working on the film eats, then the SAG actors, and lastly the nonunion actors. If you don't think it's that important to adhere to these rules, check this out. I was working on my third film as an extra. At lunchtime, after the crew had eaten, I thought I heard the person in charge say that all the rest of us could eat. I approached the buffet, which was quite appealing with baked lasagna, fish, salad, and other things. In that moment, a SAG actor stood near there, just short of yelling at us: "What are you doing?" Red-faced, he let us know that first the SAG actors eat and then we could!

I certainly don't want to poke fun at all SAG actors who do extra work, because it's a way to make a living, and if that's what one wants to do, who am I to say it's not right? It pays the bills. And besides, union actors pay dues and should rightly have some benefits over those who don't. I just thought it was funny how this particular actor went about telling us that we were wrong.

Also, as an extra, they tell you not to talk to the actors you see on the set. It makes sense, as they might be preparing, and they probably just want to help them feel comfortable during the time they're working.

My Extra Work

My parts in extra work started with being seated in the jury in the front row in a courtroom scene in a movie entitled *Pride and Loyalty* with Charles Durning, two-time Academy Award nominee. From there, I did some passes (just walking in the background) in a scene with Queen Latifa in *Life Support* and a scene as an FBI agent in a new drama with Timothy Hutton called *Kidnapped*. It was interesting to see the actors you see on TV or on the big screen work, and extra work is interesting to do at this stage of my career, but I hope that it won't be necessary later on down the road.

As you can expect, the pay was minimal: $75–$85 per day for nonunion and $120–$135 for union. Once, even though I'm nonunion, I even got $100. In addition, if you are in the union, there are extra allowances for clothing, food, and other things.

Work Ethic

I was talking to an actor friend of mine one day who does mostly voice-over work. I had told her about all the things I was doing to promote myself, and my business of being an actor and looking for work, and she said, "Boy, that's a lot of work!"

I think that if you have it in you to do whatever is necessary, it's better. If you don't, well, then you need to find the drive and discipline somewhere to do what you have to do every day. It's real simple. If you don't have a plan, it won't get done. If you don't know exactly what you're working for, how are you going to get there? And if you don't work hard, then you really can't complain that you're not getting good results.

It's tough sometimes when you get home late at night after class at 11:15 p.m., make something to eat, check your mail, and check through all the breakdowns you submit electronically for jobs. Even at midnight there might be mailings to prepare because of an audition possibility or casting you saw that day in *Backstage* or in *Show Business* or on one of the many Web sites you check twice daily. In the end, it all depends how bad you want it.

Walking All Over The City

Then there is walking all over the city all day. There were days when I had four auditions. Unfortunately, it wasn't the norm, but it happened. I often had three auditions in one day. Walking all over the city is tiring, especially when you have to carry a bag with your clothes to all the different auditions. The smarter actors have a midsize trolley suitcase that they can pull behind them all day.

I worked a lot—too much—and I should have taken more time to just rest and separate myself from the work. I was so into it, though. I couldn't stand to do nothing. But I did occasionally go to the movies and once to the theater. Looking back, though, I could maybe have rested more.

That brings me to the gym and keeping fit.

The Importance of Keeping Fit

Focusing on your craft and trying to get work is a full-time job. Everything starts with us as a human being. Flesh and blood. Mind and body. So we have to take care of ourselves. If you're tired and weak because you haven't eaten or because you haven't eaten right, that's not good.

I made it part of my schedule to get to the gym *at least* four times a week. I just felt better when I trained. Each time I went, I spent one and a half hours there doing twenty to thirty minutes of cardio; thirty to forty minutes of abs and stretching; and twenty minutes of weights, alternating biceps and lats with triceps, chest, and shoulders and legs/calves.

I also have been thinking more about my diet. To be honest, I had gotten away from that. I do drink green tea every morning, as I hear it has a lot of antioxidants. I even bought some white tea, which I haven't tasted yet, but it's supposed to be even better and healthier.

I also started eating a lot of fruit. Overall, I just *try* to eat frequently during the day, small meals that I burn off and then replenish when I need to. That keeps off excess weight.

Jamba Juice was on my schedule at least once a day. I felt a little like the Starbuck's faithfuls who have to have their café latte every morning, but I was getting my strawberry, banana, mango and blueberry smoothie after workouts.

Saying Thank You

I got into the habit of sending a postcard to casting directors after auditions just to say thank you for having me in to audition, for the callback, or for the first refusal! There are many career coaches who recommend this as well. It's just a nice touch. There were instances in which I did that and, coincidentally, the casting director or agent called me in for another audition.

The Resources I Used

I want to briefly mention some of the trade papers I used to find work. The following is a list of the trade papers that I picked up regularly, looked through, and made submissions:

- *Backstage*: comes out every Thursday morning. Get it hot off the press if you can.

- *Show Business*: comes out every Tuesday morning. Ditto.

- *Ross Reports*: monthly.

- *New York Agencies*: updated every three months. I bought it once in those three months.

- *Henderson Labels*: Extremely useful!

I also visited Reproductions to get my head shots reproduced. They also have an online contact sheet service. It has a minimal yearly cost associated with it, and you can put all your pictures on their server, choose your favorites, send the link to your agent or anyone else who can help you pick out your shots. Then they give you feedback online. Once you pick out the pictures you want printed, you can order retouching and the actual pictures all online. Reproductions isn't the only place to do this. There are others that are cheaper, but I've been happy with Reproductions' service and quality and have been using them for a couple of years now.

Recommended Reading:

I recommend reading either one or all the books on the following:

- *Sandford Meisner on Acting* by Sandford Meisner and Dennis Longwell
- *Dream of Passion* by Lee Strassberg and Evangeline Morphos
- *Respect for Acting* by Uta Hagen
- *The Art of Acting* by Stella Adler

Reading all of them will help you gain a better understanding for the different acting methods and maybe help you in your choice of schools or teachers. I also read the following books:

- *Zen in the Art of Archery* by Eugen Herrigel and Daisetz T. Suzuki
- *Live Your Dreams* by Les Brown
- *Acting as a Business* by Brian O'Neil: Gives an interesting perspective coming from a lot of experience and fact based on how to achieve success as an actor
- *The Organized Actor* by Leslie Becker: Shares her experience in creating greater clarity for the direction you've taken as an actor and provides all the templates and tools an actor needs to monitor his entire business, from audition information to financial expenditures
- *The Purple Cow* by Seth Goldwin: Speaks to how important it is to be different from all the rest. (With all the competition, we need this in our own personal marketing plans.)
- *The Seven Habits of Highly Effective People* by Stephen Covey
- *Awaken The Giant Within:* by Anthony Robbins

The Website Casting Resources I used primarily:

www.actorsaccess.com
www.nycastings.com
www.exploretalent.com

These were the Web sites that I used and checked most frequently. After doing my research and talking to some people, I decided to focus on those three. I actually got pretty good responses, especially from the first two.

I think I got only a couple of responses from the Explore Talent Web site. The site rarely had the shoot date in any of the breakdowns, which was really annoying. Actors Access and NYCastings usually have them. Another thing I didn't like was that Explore Talent has so many listings, that when you click on one listing/breakdown, you can't stay in that page and just click Next. You have to go back out to the list, find the one you want, and click on that one to go back in to another breakdown. Sounds minor, but when you have little time, you want to work as efficiently as possible. Having said all that, if I had continued my stay, I would have searched for another site to add to the first two.

In my opinion, Actors Access is the more prestigious of the three. They have very good overall services and are linked to Breakdown Services, which is the official supplier of breakdowns in the industry. You can upload two pictures for free and can upload other pictures as well for a small fee. Your agents and managers can also put up pictures of you and submit you through that Web site for projects. They also will notify you via text message on your cell phone if a casting director has sent you an e-mail in response to a submission that you did. They even send reminders—three times! Actors Access also gives you an overview of all your submissions, which are kept on file so you can review them anytime you want.

NYCastings has a very clean look, easy overview, and they let you upload five pictures. They give you the shoot dates and the pay scale, just like Actors Access. They also have good, clean, updated information and breakdowns, and a daily sheets page where you can see all the new breakdowns and castings from that particular day. Handy if you check every day.

Results Time!

So, after all that, what did I actually do for work during these three months? I will show you what I did over a nine-week period: first how many submissions I did, broken down by category; then I'll list actual auditions, callbacks, and bookings. Hopefully this type of analysis will give you some insight as to how you might analyze your own business.

Submissions by Agent #1

Type of Project	# Submissions	# Auditions/ castings	Callbacks	On Hold	Booking
Film	18	2	0	0	0
Television	12	0	0	0	0
Commercial	32	9	1	1	0
Industrial	4	3	2	1	1
Internet	2	2	0	0	0
Promo	2	1	0	0	0
Totals	70	17	3	2	1
Percentages	100% = the total # of times that the agent submitted me for projects over a nine week period	24% = % of submissions that became auditions	18% = callback rate vs. # of auditions	12% = on hold rate vs. # of auditions 66% = on hold rate vs. # of callbacks	6% = booking rate vs. # of auditions 33% = booking rate vs. # of callbacks

Considerations:

To have a chance to book any job, you have to have an audition or a chance to present yourself in some way, shape or form. So the question becomes, how can I increase that 6 percent booking rate? One sure answer would be: Stellar auditions! After four weeks and several auditions and not having any callbacks, I made some adjustments. All the callbacks on the chart with Agent 1 came after I made adjustments. They all came in a period of less than two weeks.

Other interesting observations: Only twice out of thirty times that I was submitted for projects in film and TV was I accepted to audition. Why? Not enough credits on my résumé? Probably. Wasn't right for the role? Could be. Didn't like my headshots? Could be. At any rate, I need to work on finding that out and figure out how to up that percentage. If I were staying in New York, I would definitely be working on that one.

Keeping track of your auditions helps when it comes time to analyze things that are working and things that are not. The more detail you have, the better your analysis can be and the better conclusions you can draw. I kept track of all the auditions, and I'm glad I did this. Here are some examples of some of the information I kept track of on a regular basis, thanks to Leslie Becker's book *The Organized Actor:*

Project title	Sprint
Casting director	House Productions
Location	450 W. 15th St. 2nd Floor (between 9th and 10th)
Date	June 29, 2006
Time	4:10 p.m.
Submitted by	My agent
Medium	On-camera commercial
Role	Football fan
Wardrobe	Red Football jersey and Red hat
People in the audition room	Young woman working (Cristine) the camera and giving me direction
Comments	I had to sit and act like I was watching a football game on my cell phone and react to it in a natural way. She didn't want it to be too over the top. I think I was very natural; maybe in one instant I exaggerated. The jersey probably wasn't necessary, but then again, you never know!

Here's another:

Project title	Pfizer
Casting director	Don Case Casting
Location	386 Park Ave So. Between 27th&28th Ste 809
Date	July 12, 2006
Time	2:00 p.m.
Submitted by	My agent
Medium	Industrial
Role	Self
Wardrobe	Business casual: khaki slacks, blue button-down shirt, a tie, and no jacket (I added the tie at the last minute. I felt it).
People in the audition room	Woman (Donna) from the casting office plus other man with whom I had to audition.
Comments	Shirley at the front desk. Great atmosphere in that casting office! One of my favorites. I arrived super early and got dressed, grabbed the copy, learned it, and nailed it when I went in. I felt really good, was connected to my scene partner. (This is one I got called back for.)

To be honest, there were a couple of auditions in which I didn't do well at all. I either messed up the read/text or I didn't feel natural, or my improvisation of the situation they described wasn't very good, or I wasn't in the moment. On the other hand, there were auditions I felt I nailed. I felt good and everything went smoothly. When that happened, I typically had given myself more time to prepare, arrived earlier, learned the copy, and felt more relaxed and focused, more natural and myself.

I think I take direction well and work well with adjustments. I've found that to be really important. This is a fast-paced business. People don't have much patience sometimes when they explain things to you.

The auditions in which I did the best were mostly those where I had copy to read. I did less well on commercial auditions where I was asked to improvise the entire scene. But then again, this is my perception! We never really know what the person behind the camera, the CD, or the client is really looking for, so I have learned to just make my own decisions and choices and go for it. This is what I've been taught. Just like the Iovate audition. I did a read as well as I knew how, and then I was asked to do it again with an adjustment that gave me more insight, with clear instruction as to what they wanted.

That's also why in my own submissions, I really only submit myself for jobs that I think I am spot-on for. I've met some actors who submit for anything, even if they think they might not be right for the part. I can understand why they do this, but I don't personally like that approach. Especially with important and noted casting directors, if I submit myself for projects for which I really feel right for, it is a way to build credibility with them. If the breakdowns say one thing and I submit myself anyway, I might get tossed out in the bin, and maybe they will remember me the next time there is a submission and will think, "Oh, there HE is again, trying anything and everything…" It doesn't, in my opinion, give a very professional impression of me. Also, there might be that role one day where you really feel right for the part and maybe the casting director doesn't readily see it but knows you have a good, honest track record of submitting for things you've really been right for and will feel more inclined to let you audition. You've built up your credibility with that casting director, and I think they would be more likely to give you a shot. Don't waste your chances on anything and everything and destroy your credibility. It could come back to haunt you.

In any case, I should probably work on improv and take an on-camera commercial class. I'll definitely do that next time I come back. I feel confident that I'll further improve my chances if I do that. At the very least, I'll feel even more comfortable.

In trying to analyze the numbers in that chart of submissions above, I also asked myself a few more questions:

- How to increase the rate of getting called in for auditions vs. the number of submissions: One way is to get new headshots. I found that my new color headshots got me a much higher degree of contact on submissions than did my old black and white, too cool headshots. The other thing to consider is the résumé. I don't have a lot of credits, so most of the submissions that were done on my behalf for film and television were not accepted. I have to work on that. I knew it, but I thought I'd try anyway. Brian O'Neil told me exactly what I had to do to improve my résumé and I'm working on it.

- How to increase the number of callbacks (commercials): Stellar auditions; relax, be conversational, dress the part, be on time, learn the copy, say thank you (postcard follow-up). Take an on-camera commercial class.

- How can I increase the on-hold rate: ditto; plus wear the same thing to callbacks and if possible, do the same thing (They called me back, because the liked what they saw in the first place, so don't change it. That's what I've been told by folks who have been around awhile.)

Submissions by **Agent 2**

Type of Project	# Submissions	# Auditions/ castings	Callbacks	Booking
On-Camera Commercial	?	4	0	0

I need to improve my record keeping on my online submissions. I didn't keep track of these submissions so closely. Often they were done on the run. When I saw something, I submitted myself for it without documenting it. In some cases, I submitted for the same project through different Web sites and sometimes without even realizing it. It is also possible that my agent submitted me for projects that I had also submitted myself for.

Online Submissions:

Website column key:
NYC = New York Castings
AA = Actors Access
ET = Explore Talent

Type of Project	# Submissions	# Auditions/castings	Callbacks	On Hold	Bookings	Web site
Film	15	3	1	0	0	NYC
Modeling (Print)	25	3	3	n/a	3 (got called back for 2 more jobs)	NYC
Film	11	0	0	0	0	AA
Modeling (Print)	0	0	0	0		AA
On-Camera Commercial	30	5	1	1	0	AA
Industrial	4	1	1	0	0	AA
Film	10	0	0	0	0	ET
Modeling (Print)	7	0	0	0	0	ET
Commercial	25	0	0	0	0	ET
Industrial	1	0	0	0	0	ET
Totals	135	14	7	1	3	
	100%	10% of submissions became auditions. Fifty-four percent of these came after I got new head shots	50% callback rate vs. auditions; 60% after I made my adjustments; i.e. new headshots, attitude change, etc.	14% on hold rate vs. callbacks and 7% vs. number of auditions	43% booking rate vs. callback and 21% booking rate vs. # of auditions	

That means that out of a total of some 200 submissions, I got 31 auditions and only 4 bookings! In other words:

- I auditioned for 17% of the things I was submitted for.
- I was called back for 10 out of 31 auditions I went on or 32% of the time.
- I was put on hold 10% of the time I auditioned.
- I booked 2% of the things I was submitted for.
- I booked 13% of the things I auditioned for.

Another interesting fact:

- With my agent 1, I was called into audition 24% of the time I was submitted.
- With my online submissions I was called into audition only 10% of the time.

That makes sense as the submissions through the agent are more personal and casting directors know the agents. With online submissions, I'm guessing, there is more competition with probably anyone and everyone submitting just to be submitted. Casting directors probably don't have time to sort through all the mess. This is a piece of information I would like to know more about. I'll find out and let you know.

So, what do you think about my results? Not very encouraging? I guess it depends on who you talk to. Ask me! Fortunately I was doing other things and booked things on my own, not much, but at least I did something else. I was really sorry to have to leave, because I felt like I just started to get my groove on and hit my stride!

The numbers in the table do not include certain projects I booked directly on my own, such as extra work, the photo shoots, or the job for the Learning Channel.

What do your stats look like? What other deductions can you make from my stats? This is why I tell people who are even newer to the business than I am that while it's true that I was afforded a lot of opportunities to audition and to get seen by casting directors, I also had to do other things and not just to rely on that and on what my agents were doing for me. There were weeks when I was only sent out just a few times on auditions and others when I was sent out between eight and ten times. I had to keep things going by submitting myself for projects, doing mailings, phone calls, etc., which all paid off somewhat. Now I'm smarter and know more about what to do next time!

I also did two drop-offs in this period for a *Law & Order* episode and for a game show hosting job in London. I got no response.

Summing It Up

So, when it is all said and done for this round of three months, which was really nine weeks of auditioning in New York, I can look myself in the mirror and honestly say that I did what I knew how to do to get the following results:

Paying jobs (total earnings were less than $2,000):

- One program on the Learning Channel
- One industrial for New York Life
- Three-day photo shoot for stock photos
- Three films as an extra

Close calls:

- Was called four other times to work as an extra, but I was already working
- On hold for Mercedes commercial
- On hold Put on hold for Iovate commercial
- Callback for Pfizer but I couldn't go, because it was after my departure from New York
- Called in for nine other auditions, but couldn't go because I was already working or because of a scheduling conflict.

Classes:

- Meisner technique: Ward Studio, Tuesday and Fridays from 7:30 p.m. to 10:30 p.m.
- TV hosting: Actors Connection with Pat Murphy-Stark, one Wednesday a week for four weeks
- One-day seminar with Brian O'Neil
- One private coaching session with Brian O'Neil
- One private coaching session with Leslie Becker
- One-day seminar: The Wealthy Artist with Tyrone Jackson, who teaches artists to make more money part-time using what they already know. Great class.
- One evening voice-over class with Lisa Fischoff and Elizabeth Brunell: The basics of voice-over work. Very practical, with four reads per person (there were eight of us)

I worked eight days in the three months I was in New York, but I did so much work to get those eight days! I was close to booking other jobs, but unfortunately "close" only counts when contacting casting directors when you're trying to get them to call you in for auditions. It can help raise their interest in you if you report callbacks and report being put on hold. I was fortunate enough not to have to worry about going to work, because I had saved up the money to focus on my classes and auditions. We'll get into that aspect in one of the next books.

So now let's look at my initial goals for the summer and see if I achieved them.

Goal	Done?	Comments
Meisner class for the duration of the three-month period	Yes	At the end of the three month class, I asked my teacher for a personal interview and asked for feedback.
Book an industrial and/or commercials	Yes	I asked why I was chosen. They told me that they liked my persona on-camera, they liked my little story and the personality that came out with it and they said my look was professional and exactly what they were looking for.
Take a TV hosting class sometime during the three months	Yes	Great class. Great teacher: Pat Murphy-Stark. Besides furthering my training on the teleprompter and learning how to host in different situations and with different types of text, I also learned how to pitch my own television program.
Get new color headshots.	Yes	Interesting experience. Although I was pretty satisfied with my headshots, they could be better. I deviated from my original photographer and paid the price in service. I'll know better next time. In spite of it all, the new, color shots are getting me more recognition.

Finish writing my book by the date I had set for myself	No	I actually thought I was finished, but there was something missing. It was this last section of the book, sharing what I did over these last three months. I set another date and stayed on track to get it finished.
Give input for the revamping of my business Web site www.jolten.com (Jolten Educational Events and Entertainment) so that I can begin to collect names for my courses and seminars this fall when I go back to Italy. October 15 launch.	Yes	On schedule.

There would be so much more to tell if I had only experienced it. But the purpose of this section was to show you what I did so that you might draw some conclusions as to what you might like to do for yourself. It was about giving you more information so you know what it could be like when you go at it full throttle and try to make your dreams come true. It's about helping folks realize that it is a lot of work, but with hard work come results. What if we live in this "blitz mode" of putting our nose to the grindstone for months, years? What kind of results could we get? What kind of results could you get?

Although I have been studying acting for only three years, this is the first time that I seriously went at it full-time for three months. My results were not exceptional, but they weren't bad and they did help me understand several things. This is the last and perhaps most important question: What do I take away from this experience?

I realize I was just getting started, but after just nine weeks of auditioning and working, I was really just beginning to get into my stride and build momentum. That's exciting for the next time I'm here in New York!

1. To be auditioning full-time for nine weeks, I had to first prepare the territory. I could never have just walked in and started without first letting people know I was in New York and keeping my eyes open for programs that might help me reach my goals. Well, I could have, but it would have taken longer.

2. If I work hard, I have possibilities and the capability to build a career. How big, I'm not sure, but I think I have a lot of say-so in how big it can be. Everything I have experienced leaves me with that impression.

3. My preparation before coming to New York wasn't nearly what it needed to be. Now I know. Next time things should be much smoother so I can really hit the ground running.

4. Being disciplined to work hard and continuously find ways to work smarter brings results.

5. Mailings bring results and targeted mailings bring better results.

6. Networking and building relationships with the right people bring results.

7. It is essential to learn how to deal with rejection, because it can be pretty devastating if you let it get to you. I consider myself to be extremely positive, but, I'm only human! However, I never dwell in it. Looking to the analysis always helps me. I always ask myself, "What is happening? Why is that happening and how can I make it better?"

8. I can use the fact that I was called back, put on hold or actually booked projects/work in mailings to report progress and build credibility with casting directors and agents.

9. After three months, I started to get into my rhythm. I gained momentum. I felt like I was beginning to know what I was doing, how to audition. My mailing machine was well oiled, and I was always learning things to help me get better and then applying them right away. I was building relationships and credibility with casting directors. When I did that, they began calling me personally. So I need to keep that up.

10. Having a coach or a mentor is important.

11. I must maintain those contacts that I made so I don't have to start all over again when I come back.

12. Three months is a long time to be away from my son. I'll have to do it a different way next time. I already have an idea. I need to break up the trip more and come back to Italy every now and then.

13. This experience helped me further narrow down who this book is for! I first thought to write for all artists. Too broad, I thought. Then I thought for all actors. Still too broad, because it's not for all actors. And then, after the many conversations over these past few months with young aspiring actors (of which there many and with whom I have a lot in common), I finally came to the conclusion that they, like me, need information. So I'll share what I know and hope someone else will do the same with me.

14. Without this experience in these three months, this book wouldn't be the same. It would be good, but incomplete.

15. I got better as an actor and performer in general. I feel good about that. I also realize that there are things I need to work on. Talking to my teacher, straight up, face to face about that helped me understand those things even more than just being in class.

16. Seeing my classmates work can teach you a lot!

17. I have the potential to succeed! I will make it!

So there you have it! Now here are some questions for you:

- What would *you* take away from this experience over the three-month period as I reported it if it had been you living it instead of me?

- What would *you* have done differently if you had been in my shoes?

- What will *you* do if you encounter some of the same situations?

- How do *you* think you will fare if you do what I did? Why?

- Why do *you* think I got the results I did?

- What do *you* think I will have to do to get better results?

Next Steps

So what are my next steps?

1. Priority number one: Finish writing the book and get it to the editor.

2. Brian O'Neil helped me put together a plan that will help me expand what I have built in New York and position myself for further success when I return. I will be implementing that over the next six months. In fact, I'm in the process of writing some seventy-five postcards to my contacts in New York, which is part of the plan.

3. In the meantime, I will focus on my mission: "Make the most money in the least amount of time, with the least amount of effort, so that I have more time to focus on my craft." This way I can return to New York early next year as planned to take my next level of Meisner, further this book project, and audition more.

4. In line with that mission, my business consultancy Web site (www.jolten.com) is being revamped to position me to do more open seminars for business and private people alike. If you want to have a chuckle, go to www.lavitachevorrei.it and hear me speak Italian!

I sincerely hope that this section has been informative. Again, it's not about evaluating me; it's about stimulating you to raise your head every now and then and take stock of what you are doing. Analyze your results and figure out what works and what doesn't and fix it. Talk to other actors, but ask good questions and take notes. I worked my ass off. I tell you this because it can be a full-time job if you want it to be. There is always something to do. Always! Could I have worked smarter? Now I know that I could have, and I will going forward. We never stop learning.   Most of all, though, this book is about giving you the information you are hungry for and is written by someone who took the time to tell you how it is. This information isn't coming from someone who is already super successful. I will be, but I'm not yet! I'm just like you. I'm learning too.

In the end, I guess it all depends on who you are, how good you are, what you look like, how well you know yourself, how you market yourself, how you communicate, how dedicated you are, what you're willing to do to get where you want to go, what you have on your résumé, how much training you have, your work ethic, whether you're into training, how much drive and determination you have, how disciplined you are, how you persevere, how much you believe it's possible for you to achieve what you want, how well you handle rejection, how giving you are, how professional you are, how punctual you are, how objective you are, how humble and willing to learn you are, how much you are willing to sacrifice, the kind of people you surround yourself with, your ability to plan and to see the future and what you want. It depends on a lot of things. And then there's a dose of luck that we can't forget about either.

Nike calls it *innovation*, Bernard Hiller calls it the *pink elephant*, Seth Godin calls it the *Purple Cow*, and I call it *the Short Line Strategy*. Those four things all have something in common. What's the common thread? That's a whole other book! I will tell you, however, that this book you are finishing right now is part of that short line philosophy, so stay tuned.

CHAPTER 14

Final Thoughts

There's a lot of information in this book. If you went through the exercises that were designed to stimulate thought and help you on your way, then you should be pretty far along in gaining more clarity around what you want and how you intend to achieve it.

If you are not used to this way of thinking, it might take some getting used to. It can be a bit overwhelming. If this is the case for you, just go someplace quiet, take a couple of deep breaths, relax, and think about what it is you really want. Think about the future you will have when you achieve your goals. Remember that your plan is a living plan, which means that it can be changed, adjusted, modified, shifted. Do this until you feel really comfortable with it. It might take days, weeks, months, but don't stop asking yourself until you get a crystal clear answer.

Think about why you want what you want. That's where your motivation to persevere comes from. If it is strong, you will continue. You must be passionate. You must love your goal!

In your different achievement areas in life, think about why you chose certain ones and why you decided to concentrate on them first. Go over it again just long enough to feel comfortable with your decisions.

I believe goals are important, but don't get so caught up in them that you lose focus of what is important today. Acting teaches us that nailing a scene isn't the objective. We must be present in each and every moment of the scene for it to be real and interesting to our audience. Be in the moment. Enjoy your journey and enjoy the life you have chosen.

Take care of yourself. Celebrate your victories, your successes. Remember that bigger goals are comprised of a series of smaller ones. Take time to pause and reflect on what went well and what didn't, but also to enjoy what you have achieved to date. Don't be all work and no play. Treat yourself for your hard work. Rest. Exercise. Nurture your relationships with friends and family and loved ones. These things are important to give you the fuel you need to continue on your journey.

Don't forget your language! If you need to, go back and revisit the chapter about the importance of asking yourself questions. They can make you or break you. Focus on the solutions and not the problems.

Remember to stay positive. The bigger and more ambitious your goals, the more likely it is that at some point along your way, you will run into obstacles, situations that will be difficult to resolve, and sometimes you will make mistakes. Someone once said that every mistake is an opportunity to become more intelligent. An ex-colleague of mine, Trevor Edwards, said, "Without risk, there is no genius." Be courageous and dare to be huge. Keep the negative people at a distance and don't let them get under your skin. Stick to what you believe in and go for it!

I sincerely hope that you have found in these pages more clarity of purpose, more motivation, vision, a method for your planning, some wisdom and inspiration.

Whatever it is you are striving for, don't stop until you get it!

~~The End~~
The Beginning

I will leave you with my favorite paragraph in this entire book. It is my favorite because it sums up my reason for being. It lets me know that what I am doing is right. It also lets me know that I will succeed! I hope that you experience what it feels like to write a paragraph like this for yourself. It's such a great feeling!

So, I can say that this book and the rest of this project that I have created gives me that chance that I have created for myself to be able to practice my acting on video, write, help others, promote myself and others, rediscover parts of myself, learn about the industry, communicate to a large audience, create opportunities for myself and for others, put myself on the line, have fun, have the flexibility I need to concentrate on developing my craft, make a living doing something I love, spend time with my son, learn, make a difference, tell stories, dream, have an audience, perform, innovate, express myself, challenge myself, study, blow off steam, develop my creativity, explore, be myself, grow, give, be humble, share, positively affect people's lives, meet the right people to further my career, audition, reach my goals, make money, teach my son how to make money, make new friends, believe that what I want is possible, lead, be an example, work, and prepare myself for an inevitable evolution and creation of my own timeline of innovation.

Go for what you want and don't stop until you get it! Do it now and don't wait until tomorrow.

The best way to predict your future is to create it.

Anonymous

Good luck to you, and God bless.

APPENDIX

Key to the 9 dot exercise on page 63

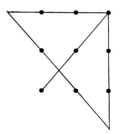

978-0-595-41902-9
0-595-41902-X

Lightning Source UK Ltd.
Milton Keynes UK
UKOW051713081011

180001UK00001B/47/A